The Future of Enterprise Applications

The Future of Enterprise Applications

Series Editor
Bruce Richardson

Edition Editor
Jim Shepherd

Editor
Randy Weston

AMR Research

To request permission to use parts of this book or order copies, contact the director of publications at bookreprints@amrresearch.com, or write to AMR Research, 125 Summer Street, Fourth Floor, Boston MA 02110-1616. Telephone: 617.542.6600, 8:30 a.m. to 5:30 p.m. ET, Monday through Friday. Fax: 617.542.5670.

Library of Congress Data
The future of enterprise applications.
    Includes index.
    ISBN 0-9785928-1-6

                                                                2006936574
                                                                      LCCN

Printed in the United States of America
10 9 8 7 6 5 4 3 2 1

This book is printed on 100% post-consumer recycled fiber. It is manufactured entirely with wind-generated electricity and in accordance with a Forest Stewardship Council (FSC) pilot program that certifies products made with high percentages of post-consumer reclaimed materials.

Table of Contents

Preface   VII

Introduction   XI

The State of the Enterprise Application Market

The Enterprise Application Market Is Destroying
   Its Fragile Ecosystem   7
Follow the Money: The New Era of Private Equity
   Enterprise Applications   15
Innovation in the New Enterprise Application Market   25

The Disruptive Effect of Technology

Service-Oriented Architectures:
   Business Needs First, Technology Second   35
Wikis and Blogs: New Collaboration Tools Force Change   47
Web 2.0   55
The New Role of Portals   61

Planning for SOA and the New World of Composite Applications

Overcoming the Hurdles   71
The Governance and People Hurdle   75
The Process Hurdle   81
The Technology and IT Governance Hurdle   87

New Delivery Models and Licensing in the Software Industry

State of the Union for License Software Models   97
State of the Union for the SaaS Model   105
The Software Buyer   111

V

The New Role of Service Providers and System Integrators

ERP Consultants and Service Providers:
    Take Care Along the Multivendor Sourcing Path   121

India's Role in Global ERP and SOA Services   125

The Future: Enterprise Applications in 2010 and Beyond

Safety First   135

The Death of Packaged Software   139

Appendix: Enterprise Application Markets

Enterprise Resource Planning   149

Human Capital Management   155

Business Intelligence and Performance Management   163

Supply Chain Management   171

Supply Management: Procurement and Sourcing   179

Customer Relationship Management   185

Service Lifecycle Management   191

B2B E-Business   199

Product Lifecycle Management   205

Manufacturing Operations   211

Retail Enterprise Applications   219

Acronyms and Initialisms   227

Index   229

Contributors   241

About AMR Research   243

Preface

Enterprise applications have become much more than just software. In addition to supporting most commercial transactions, they are also the primary source of business data, vital to regulatory compliance, and one of the most valuable assets to a company.

Business applications first emerged forty years ago as simple electronic filing cabinets and calculators. As computing technology improved and programming skills developed, these applications became increasingly sophisticated, expanding to support most parts of the business. In the early 1980s, innovative software vendors began to build integrated sets of departmental applications on a central database, and the first enterprise applications were born. Since then, hundreds of thousands have been sold and deployed around the world.

This success has turned the enterprise application market into a major industry, with software vendors generating more than $50 billion in annual revenue and making use of at least $200 billion in associated hardware, infrastructure, and IT services sales by their partners. Hardware vendors used to view applications as "loss leaders" to entice companies to buy computers, but now enterprise applications represent the heart of most companies' IT strategies, dictating or heavily influencing nearly all IT decisions.

Most corporations today cannot operate without their enterprise applications. This software no longer simply supports activities and records data, it is the way business is done. Whether it's customers entering their own sales orders, accountants closing the month, or products being shipped from a warehouse, there is no manual way to perform these transactions anymore. The complexity of modern business and the required velocity of activities demand the use of highly sophisticated applications and powerful computing platforms. This growing dependency on enterprise applications has made decisions such as vendor selection, deployment sequence, and upgrade timing highly strategic. In many organizations, these issues have now been elevated to executive management committees or even the board of directors because of their sensitivity and potential impact on the business.

AMR Research has written *The Future of Enterprise Applications* because we recognize how important these decisions have become to businesses and how difficult it can be to understand the highly dynamic enterprise application landscape. Armed with the largest team of analysts covering these applications, we have assembled their best thinking on the major trends and influences in the industry.

Chapter 1 looks at the rapid consolidation and restructuring now taking place in the enterprise application market. We not only examine why it is happening, but also look at the potential impact on innovation if the environment becomes too hostile to support niche and startup vendors. We also discuss the recent involvement of private equity firm funding, which is leading the rollup of small and midsize software vendors. AMR Research believes that it is crucial for companies to understand who their application vendor really is and what their mid- and long-term business strategy is likely to be.

The introduction of service-oriented architectures is having a disruptive impact on the enterprise application market. Chapter 2 delves into why they are becoming important to customers and what the major vendors are doing with them. We also look at other new and potentially disruptive technologies, like wikis and blogs, and how companies are addressing their use. Chapter 3 takes on the growing trend toward using these technologies for custom development as well as the emergence of composite applications and business process management.

Chapter 4 focuses on new software delivery and purchasing models, particularly the growing interest in approaches such as on demand and software as a service. We also look at what vendors are currently offering and some of the likely scenarios for the market over the next several years. In Chapter 5, we look at the system integrators and IT service providers that serve the enterprise application market, including the growing trend for customers to outsource significant parts of the implementation and support to these firms. We also look at the significant changes among the provider landscape, specifically at the Indian service providers and the efforts that the traditional Tier 1 firms are making to provide global delivery options.

Chapter 6 considers the enterprise application market over the next five years and offers two very different scenarios for what might happen. My view is that the market will evolve along familiar lines, constrained by the inherent conservatism of enterprise buyers. Bruce Richardson, AMR Research's chief research officer, argues that new technologies and the influence of more dynamic markets, like Web 2.0, will change everything, believing the enterprise application market of 2010 will look nothing like the one today.

The Appendix covers 11 enterprise application market segments, ranging from enterprise resource planning to retail applications. For each segment, we present a market overview, market-sizing and momentum data, a list of the leading vendors, and brief looks at the major influences and likely futures. This is not intended as a comprehensive analysis, but rather a high-level guide for managers that need to gain a general understanding of these markets.

The Future of Enterprise Applications is designed to serve as a useful reference book for executives and practitioners that are faced with difficult decisions about these highly strategic products. We have tried to provide a broad perspective on this market to help buyers understand the current trends and how those may affect them or their vendors in the next few years. We also hope that the book will provoke discussion within the reader's organization and dialog with AMR Research.

We are passionately interested in enterprise applications. For 20 years, we have been helping companies understand and use them to improve their business processes. We hope this book will help businesses realize even more value from their investments in these powerful products.

Jim Shepherd
October 2006

Introduction

From 1995 until 2001, $170 billion in private equity funded more than 20,000 startups, with another $125 billion raised from 1,300 IPOs. While $2 trillion in wealth was subsequently lost in capital markets, core industry has increasingly benefited by deploying the technologies that these lost investments funded:

- The Internet has become part of our social and business fabric.

- Global fiber-optic and wireless infrastructures were put in place, which have fueled industrialization from Boston to Bangalore to Belarus.

- Every imaginable component of business application functionality was developed and introduced. This industry has gone from an emergence phase a decade ago to a $51 billion market in 2005.

- Hardware price/performance dramatically improved.

- Business process and integration standards were established.

These technological advances have shifted the basis of competition across all industries and have accelerated a business transformation that is creating a few winners in every industry—and a large number of losers. As this happens, the once vibrant technology industry that aided these advances is undergoing rampant consolidation. The result is a few large technology suppliers, like IBM, Microsoft, Oracle, and SAP, and an absence of new venture-funded, innovative, best-of-breed challengers. There is a growing belief that without these emerging challengers, innovation will suffer.

Real innovation in business will not be more product or features development, but in process innovation or the deployment of technology. This will be aided by technology advancements like service-oriented architectures (SOAs) and new business models like software as a service (SaaS)—technologies and models that are designed with the business needs in mind.

In Lou Gerstner's farewell letter to IBM employees and shareholders published as the Chairman's letter of the IBM 2001 Annual Report, he said: "Approximately half the investments that customers make in IT are now driven by line-of-business managers, not chief information officers. This is a remarkable shift in just five or six years.

Not that CIOs have become unimportant. They now sit at the table where technology is translated into business value. And their traditional bailiwick of infrastructure, too, has been transformed by the networked world. But there's no question that business strategy now sets the technology agenda, not the other way around."

In meeting these demands, the old enterprise application model won't work—it doesn't leave enough room in the budget for real innovation of business processes. 70% of IT investment is in base technology. Most of the remaining 30% supports functions that don't add much value, like maintenance and customization. This huge portion of IT spending is indistinguishable and will become a utility over time—thus the trend toward outsourcing, offshoring, and hosted systems, which will grow significantly in the coming years to create massive IT utility companies. To meet changing business needs, these utilities will need to be more flexible. This is where disruptive technologies like SOAs enter the picture, and why the future of the enterprise application market rides so much on how these technologies take root.

In the end, IT innovation to a business is defined by how technology strengthens business process advantages. It's not innovation alone that makes companies winners, but how they manage processes like global supply chain management and demand-driven innovation. To companies that do these things well, IT is a powerful aid that offers productivity advantages. While the maturing of the technology industry may be a negative for investors that benefited during the product innovation boom, it is a major positive for business leaders. These executives now have a stable set of products provided by financially sound suppliers they can count on for the long term. It's now up to the technologists to make sure they can adapt to meet the business needs.

Tony Friscia
President and CEO
AMR Research

The Future of Enterprise Applications

The State of the Enterprise Application Market 1

The State of the Enterprise Application Market

On the surface, the enterprise application market looks remarkably healthy. It passed the $50 billion revenue mark in 2005, and the leading vendors—SAP, Oracle, Sage, UGS, and Microsoft—are all growing at double-digit rates. Peel back the surface, though, and you find that the success of these giant global players is not indicative of the state of the market.

Radical consolidation, several years of recession, and a major change in corporate buying preferences have combined to stunt the growth of most of the smaller software firms that once drove much of the industry's vibrancy and innovation. These companies, which have traditionally distinguished themselves on the basis of vertical, functional, or geographic specialization, simply don't seem to be participating in the economic recovery.

Where is innovation going to come from in this new application future? Can innovation thrive in a world funded by private equity? These issues will have a major impact on how and why companies buy business software. In this chapter, we look at the new models, how new investors, like private equity firms, are shaping the market, and where the market might be heading as these forces play out.

The Enterprise Application Market Is Destroying Its Fragile Ecosystem

PART ONE

The application software market needs to undergo a significant restructuring in order to breathe life back into the specialty, or best-of-breed, segment and reinvigorate the formation of new companies.

One of the wonderful things about the application software industry has always been the low barrier to entry. Anybody with a new idea, a PC, and some programming skill could start a software business. By the end of the 1990s, it felt like nearly everybody had. The growth potential and high returns from enterprise applications attracted thousands of entrepreneurs and billions of dollars of venture funding.

What happened to best of breed?

This convergence of capital and talent spawned whole application categories, like customer relationship management (CRM) and supply chain planning (SCP), and hundreds of niche applications that supported specific vertical industry needs or aided new business models and processes. The established software vendors seemed unable to keep pace with the rapid changes in areas like e-commerce, supply chain management (SCM), and global sourcing. It was the small startup vendors that supported much of the innovation.

These specialist vendors were the poster children of the Internet bubble, with unbelievable growth rates and stratospheric market valuations. Software buyers got caught up in the enthusiasm, and many companies adopted what became known as best-of-breed IT strategies, based on the notion that they could quickly assemble enterprise-wide systems by integrating a group of smaller special-purpose applications.

The prevailing wisdom was that huge enterprise resource planning (ERP) deployments were too slow and expensive, and that niche vendors offered the speed and flexibility necessary to respond to the modern business environment. The widespread assumption was that advances in technology and industry standards meant that integration would no longer be a prohibitive issue. There was little concern about the viability of software companies with huge market caps.

Then the bubble burst. The stock market plummeted, the venture capital firms retreated, and demand for software simply disappeared. The large suite vendors lived off of their huge installed bases and broad product portfolios. Small software companies, however, typically with only one product to sell, had no one left to sell to.

ERP vendors also began to cut off the oxygen to the niche firms by closing the functionality gaps in their suites through a combination of acquisitions, internal development, and improved marketing. At the same time, the global recession was changing the behavior of enterprise software buyers. IT budgets were slashed, decisions became more centralized, and everyone became more risk averse. With the acquisitions of large players like JD Edwards and PeopleSoft, and the collapse of high-flying companies like i2 Technologies and Commerce One, a best-of-breed IT strategy began to seem far too dangerous for most post-recession CIOs.

Will the consolidation continue?

High-profile acquisitions tend to make the headlines, but the real story of the enterprise software market is the market share consolidation and the power and control that it confers on the largest vendors. In the ERP space, which is roughly half of the market, SAP and Oracle have gone from 44 percent combined market share in 1999 to more than 65 percent share in 2006. At Software 2006, former Oracle president Ray Lane, now a venture capitalist, stated that 85 percent of revenue in the software industry is generated by 15 companies, 80 percent of profit is in three companies, and 50 percent of profit in one company (Microsoft).

Companies like SAP, Oracle, and Microsoft, plus other large vendors like Infor, Lawson, and Epicor, have successfully sold the concept of a single vendor integrated suite. This limits the opportunities for specialist vendors and is beginning to even erode their installed bases.

Buyers aren't showing any signs that they will move back toward best-of-breed strategies anytime soon. The major vendors have even accelerated the consolidation through aggressive acquisition strategies. Oracle alone bought more than a dozen software companies between 2004 and 2006, including the top customer management vendor (Siebel) and the No. 3 enterprise suite vendor (PeopleSoft, which had just bought No. 4 JD Edwards).

Nearly all the suite vendors use the strategy of acquisition to fill holes in their products because it is faster and more cost effective than internal development. Many of them also see acquisitions as a way to enter new markets, expand customer bases, and gain the critical mass necessary to remain competitive in a market where size matters. This has resulted in huge size and resource disparities between the few large vendors and everybody else. It has also fueled CIO fears about the viability of smaller specialty vendors.

9

Why the giant suite vendors need healthy ecosystems

One of the ironies of the enterprise application market is that the major suite vendors, especially SAP and Oracle, are now trying to court the very companies they have spent the past decade trying to destroy. As these ERP vendors reposition themselves as platform providers, they are intent on building ecosystems of independent software companies that use their underlying technology. Here are some of the reasons for this intense competition for partners:

- Endorsement of the architecture and technology vision
- Specialized functionality to fill out vertical industry systems
- Service-oriented architectures (SOAs) that aid the development of composite applications and business processes that span multiple vendor products (see chapters 2 and 3)
- A stable of potential acquisitions that are technologically compatible
- Software revenue from technology usage or resale
- A source of innovative new applications

As the market for enterprise applications matures, the buyers are expecting complete systems for their specific industry, geography, and size. In many cases, their concept of what this means includes highly specialized functionality that is not practical for the suite vendors to build because of the expertise required and the limited potential return. The suite vendors need these partners to work with them to develop these systems, and they are beginning to understand that it is very important that third-party software vendors are healthy. Customers are looking for 10- to 15-year lifecycles. Ultimately, they will hold the major suite vendor responsible for the entire system, regardless of who developed the code.

The problem with today's enterprise application market is that the control and revenue are far too concentrated in a small group of global suite vendors. This results in an ecosystem that is very weak, and stands as a barrier for new software businesses. As Darlene Mann, CEO of Siperian, points out, venture capital firms have lost interest in funding enterprise application companies because they don't see much opportunity for growth. If this continues, it will eventually impair the industry's ability to respond to changes in user expectations, business models, and technology. Most damaging, it will severely limit the flow of software-based innovation, which nearly always comes from small startup organizations.

A Conversation With Siperian's Darlene Mann

Darlene Mann, CEO of customer data integration vendor Siperian, is also a former venture capitalist. Having been on both sides of the VC fence, she has some interesting ideas on the state of innovation in the enterprise software market.

Q: Where do you see the major source of innovation in the software market coming from?

A: Innovation is still coming from the entrepreneurial community. If you look at what the big guys are doing, it's all very predictable. What has changed is that the big guys watch what the entrepreneurial community is doing and jump on innovative ideas more quickly by buying companies or adding features to their products.

The other place that is important for innovation is standards organization, though the pace is glacial. They are creating infrastructure standards that allow for more innovation. The entrepreneurial community can build its innovative ideas on the standard, such as BPEL, RSS, and such. There is less risk because they don't have to build the infrastructure. It's creating a bedrock on which one *can* innovate. I have a hard time saying it, but the value of a Microsoft or an IBM is also that they give you a platform to build on.

Q: How does an entrepreneur with an innovative idea get started today?

A: There are two different ways people come at entrepreneurship today. One is that they are bound and determined to become an entrepreneur, and they go searching for the idea. The process becomes one of searching and winnowing through ideas until they find one that can be funded. This approach is very common in Silicon Valley because of its history of software entrepreneurs. If you are a software executive and haven't done a startup, something is missing—it's almost expected of you.

People in a position to recognize an opportunity are often inside large companies and see a need not served in the customer base that is not apparent or not yet important to the large company. The market for business activity monitoring, business intelligence, and systems management tools are good examples of where opportunities happen.

As to the "how" part of the question, most startups today are small bootstrap operations because of difficulty getting VC funding. The VCs are not too interested in software. And though I don't necessarily agree, there is an anti-VC attitude among many entrepreneurs. After their experiences over the last 10 years, many entrepreneurs think VCs can do more harm than good, and that the level of control they exact in return for their money creates too much risk for the founders to welcome their involvement.

Q: How do the evolving ecosystems of the major vendors change the dynamics?

A: The big issue is how these vendors would have the community unfold. They want to capture the bulk of the revenue, and the community gets the crumbs. You can't build a big enough company off what they are leaving behind to get investors interested. If you discover a richer opportunity, the big vendors will muscle in and take it over, either buying you as their advanced development team or just doing it themselves.

Because of this, all the venture activity is in Web 2.0 startups and similar areas where the big companies don't dominate. These are mostly consumer-facing opportunities where the web infrastructure is part of the play and away from enterprise software. Even funding for software as a service is drying up, except those targeted at small business, because the big companies are moving in.

AMR Research is already hearing complaints from larger, more sophisticated users of enterprise applications that they are no longer seeing new ideas and new products in this market. The major vendors all say that they are trying to facilitate innovation with their shift to SOA and their investments in partner and developer programs, platforms, service libraries, and standards adoption. However, they are ignoring one critical factor: they don't leave any money on the table for those partners.

As most complex product industries mature, the large original equipment manufacturers (OEMs) become less vertically integrated. They allow more and more of the product to be built by their suppliers, like in the high-tech, automotive, and A&D markets. This creates a flow of revenue down the food chain that sustains a healthy ecosystem, with the suppliers becoming a critical element in product innovation and business efficiency. That has never happened in the application software industry, but it needs to soon.

The major vendors have to recognize that unless they begin to alter the structure of the industry and create a real opportunity for smaller players, they will inevitably become victims of their own success. If application buyers have to go outside the ecosystem for innovation, the entire concept of enterprise suites could crumble.

Follow the Money: The New Era of Private Equity Enterprise Applications

Everyone knows about the rapid consolidation occurring in the enterprise software market. CIOs are now accustomed to frequent ownership changes among their application vendors, but most assume it simply signifies a maturing software industry in which larger vendors buy up smaller ones to fill holes in their product lines, gain entry to new markets, or build critical mass. Oracle's multitude of acquisitions are solid evidence of this.

But something more is happening—something that may have very different implications for application buyers. Private equity firms have been spending billions to buy up software companies and combine them into very large portfolio businesses. While this may not necessarily be a threat to the industry, software owners and buyers should be aware of the ownership structure of their most important vendors. After all, the strategies and goals of investment fund managers are quite different than those of traditional software entrepreneurs.

At first glance, it may not be easy to distinguish whether your software vendor is simply borrowing some money to purchase additional functionality, or being used by one or more private equity firms as a vehicle to accumulate multiple businesses. While nearly every acquisition is positioned as one software company buying another, it may not be that simple. If the acquiring company is owned or controlled by a private equity firm, there is a good chance that the transaction has more to do with investment strategy than application synergy. Should that make a difference to the customer?

Here's the good news:

- The vendor becomes part of a larger company with more resources.

- The private equity backers are financially savvy and have deep pockets.

- The new owner is likely to be more financially viable, and may have broader geographic coverage.

- The new owner is very interested in the installed base maintenance stream, and will focus on keeping existing customers happy.

- Private equity firms are often very good at trimming costs and improving operations.

Now, the bad news:

- The real owners are financial investors with little interest in (or knowledge of) the software products or underlying technology.

- Private equity firms typically do not want to hold an investment for more than five to seven years.

- Employee, product, or customer loyalty is unlikely to influence business strategy.

- Debt reduction is a much higher priority than long-term product investments, such as functional rewrites or new architectures.

Software buyers need to understand who really owns their vendors. They should determine whether those owners are motivated to build a world-class software company with long-term customer relationships, or if their investment plans are simply to exit within a few years with a good financial return. This knowledge can be helpful in anticipating the software vendor's behavior or interpreting its announcements and promises. The nature of ownership should also be an important factor as CIOs consider the risk profile and potential volatility of their major software suppliers.

Who are the players?

Throughout the 1980s and 1990s, most software companies were started with and nurtured on venture capital. While VC firms are still funding software startups, a set of private equity investors has joined them, buying up mature software companies or taking public companies private.

In some cases, these firms manage a portfolio of independent software companies much as the venture capitalists have done. A small group of private equity firms, including Golden Gate Capital, Francisco Partners, and Thoma Cressey Equity Partners, have taken a much more aggressive approach. They select one of their portfolio companies to use as an aggregator vendor, and then acquire companies at a brisk pace to create new mega-vendors with financial resources, customer bases, and product footprints on par with some of the biggest traditional enterprise application companies (see Table 1).

Perhaps the best example of this technique is Infor, which is primarily funded by Golden Gate Capital. Infor was created though the buyout of a small process ERP system provider, Adage, and an auto supplier ERP system vendor, BRAIN. In four years of furious mergers and acquisitions, Infor has ballooned to more than $2 billion in revenue and 70,000 customers from $100 million in annual revenue and 2,000 customers.

Aggregator	Private Equity Investors	Acquired Companies	Customers
Infor	Golden Gate Capital	Adage, Aperum, Baan, BRAIN, Concerto Software, D&B Software, daly.commerce, EXE, Frontstep, Future 3, Incodev, Infinium, Infor, JBA, Lilly Software Associates, MAPICS, Marcam, Mercia, NxTrend, SCT, SSA Global, Systems Union, Varial	70,000+
Ecometry	Golden Gate Capital	ADS Retail, Blue Martini, Ecometry	500+
Attachmate	Francisco Partners, Golden Gate Capital, Thoma Cressey Equity Partners	Attachmate, NetIQ, OnDemand Software, WRQ	40,000+
RedPrairie	Francisco Partners	BlueCube Software, Marc Global, RedPrairie	27,000+ sites
GXS	Francisco Partners	G International, GXS, Haht Commerce	40,000+ sites
JDA	Thoma Cressey Equity Partners	JDA, Manugistics	5,500+
Made2Manage (M2M Holdings)	Thoma Cressey Equity Partners, Battery Ventures VI	AXIS Computer Systems, Capri, DTR Software, Encompix, Intuitive Manufacturing Systems, Made2Manage, Onyx	4,300

Table 1: Selected enterprise application aggregators and their private equity investors

Where the Money Goes

Of the more than 3,000 domestic and international venture capital and private equity firms, about 380 focus on software and software services. According to PricewaterhouseCoopers and the National Venture Capital Association, the software sector continues to lead all other sectors, even biotech, in terms of venture capital investment. In the second quarter of 2006, venture capitalists invested $1.26 billion in 231 deals, compared with more than $1.31 billion in 215 deals the previous quarter and $1.32 billion in 240 deals a year earlier in the second quarter of 2005. And this money is not funding pipe dreams in garages. Seed and startup investment accounted for about $46 million, and early-stage investment tallied about $128 million. By contrast, expansion-stage investments were a whopping $579 million, and later-stage investments were $511 million in the quarter.

New business strategies

Unlike traditional software companies using acquisitions to round out a product set or enter a new market, the aggregators are focused on scale. In order to compete with SAP, Microsoft, and Oracle in terms of investment, global reach, and product breadth, scale is essential. Most of the smaller companies acquired by these aggregators were struggling against the big players, but enclosed within a larger, well-financed organization, the acquired products can more effectively compete.

This type of consolidation, however, unfortunately comes at a price that customers must pay. By acquiring many competing products, aggregators tend to reduce competition within a market and cast the pall of acquisition over the remaining players. Because it is very expensive for customers to switch their enterprise applications, most companies have little choice but to stay put, pay maintenance, and hope for the best. While they may have had great leverage with the small vendor that originally sold them their software, they have little pull with their aggregator today.

Money makes the whole thing work. Aggregators must find a way to pay the debts they acquired to finance their expansion; generating cash flow to service their debt is essential. Cutting costs and focusing investments on only the most productive sectors and maintenance revenue help to generate that cash flow, but it can come at the expense of customer service and product enhancements. Beyond debt reduction and operation improvements, aggregators also owe their private equity firms a strong return on their investments in a relatively short time frame.

Content management, CRM, and HCM among the winners

Some software segments are clearly targets of private equity and VC investors (see Figure 1). Security software investment far outpace other segments at $222 million in investments, or about 18 percent of total investment, followed by wireless at $97 million, content management at $94 million, human capital management (HCM) and CRM at $87 million, and healthcare at $84 million. Systems management software is next on the list at $61 million, followed by product lifecycle management (PLM) investment at $50 million. Those security companies receiving the most money target network security, defense, and risk management.

Advances in mobile technology, such as the development of mobile communications software and mobile device software management, dominated the wireless space. Search and content aggregation appear to be the focus of much of the investment in content management firms, while safeguarding the pharmaceutical industry stood out among healthcare investments. In the PLM space, many vendors are developing electronic design automation software.

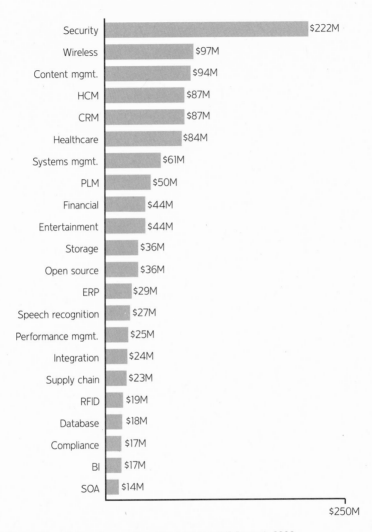

Source: PricewaterhouseCoopers MoneyTree report and AMR Research, 2006

Figure 1: Selected venture capital software segment investments

Private Equity and the IT Services Market

Thomson Financial reports that buyout funds raised $131 billion in 2005, twice the amount raised in 2004. 2006 looks set to break a number of previous records, having already witnessed the largest leveraged buyout in history with the $33 billion HCA deal that took the hospital operator private. This flood of investment has been accompanied by financial buyers' intense interest in outsourcing as a tool to realize expected returns within accelerated time frames. Service providers, understandably, have intense interest, as well. This is an obvious and rich vein to tap for outsourcing and advisory services in a marketplace that, while growing, gets more competitive every year.

Relentless mergers and acquisitions are also a catalyst for increased information technology outsourcing and business process outsourcing spending. For example, in an outsourcing deal with IBM, executives from retailer CVS remarked that while they expected "efficiencies," cost was not the primary factor behind the 10-year deal—sustained M&A activity was. In just the past two years, CVS has added 55,000 employees. Getting all those people on board, not to mention the thousands more joining from future acquisitions, demands an industrial approach to human resources operations. Enter IBM.

A number of managing partners at the largest global services companies have said that private equity and M&A are driving the bulk of their businesses today. The private equity/outsourcing dynamic, in particular, presents an opportunity but also a challenge for service providers. A financial buyer is likely to have higher expectations of what can be achieved within a shorter time frame than a business buyer might. In both cases, the devil is in the execution details, which is why firms like Deloitte (from an advisory and operational consulting perspective) and Accenture (from a consulting and outsourcing perspective) are poised to benefit.

22

How do the investors get out?

Private equity firms are particularly private about their business plans, so a question remains unanswered: what is their exit strategy? Software companies traditionally repaid their investors through an IPO, but those have become quite rare in the application software space.

SSA Global, an early aggregator funded by Cerberus and General Atlantic Partners, was one of the few enterprise application companies to go public since the bubble burst. The much-anticipated public offering took place on May 26, 2005, at $11 per share, and was valued at around $800 million. The stock price peaked at $20.58 in late 2005, but slumped back to around $15 until May 2006 when Golden Gate Capital took SSA Global private again. While the SSA Global investors probably did very well, the general feeling in the investment community is that the IPO market is not very receptive to software companies.

The most obvious way for these private equity firms to make a return on their investment is to sell off these newly aggregated software businesses, but who can they sell them to? Because they typically consist of broad product portfolios that at best are only marginally integrated, no software vendor is going buy them to fill product holes. One possibility is to follow the SSA Global route and sell them to even more aggressive aggregators, but that seems like an awfully limited potential market. The only plan that seems to make sense is to sell them to the very large software vendors: IBM, Microsoft, Oracle, or SAP.

This suggests that the real strategy at work is not about products, but about packaging up huge customer bases. Large software vendors are unlikely to be interested in a collection of older product lines with redundant functionality. They might very well be interested in ready-made, lucrative customer bases, though. Customers and prospects are notoriously difficult and expensive to get through traditional sales channels, so why not simply buy them? Perhaps these aggregators are being formed to package up attractive sets of customers along with a profitable maintenance stream and attractive long-term sales potential. The larger software vendors might not want to go through the unpleasant process of combining lots of different businesses, closing facilities, reducing head count, or reconciling support plans. However, once the dirty work is done, they become much more interesting.

We don't know how much Golden Gate has invested in Infor to accumulate 70,000 customers, but we do know that the price of customers has gone up dramatically. In 2003, Mike Greenough, then CEO of SSA Global, said that his company had paid an average of $23,500 per customer to acquire 16,000 customers. Three years later, Golden Gate paid approximately $130,000 per customer in order to merge SSA Global with Infor. This might seem expensive, but AMR Research estimates that SSA Global was generating between $40,000 and $50,000 in annual revenue per customer.

Would a large software vendor be interested in buying cleaned-up, prepackaged customer bases? We think so. Oracle acknowledged from the beginning that its primary motivation in buying PeopleSoft was to get the customer base; it already had an ERP system it believed was superior. Microsoft didn't buy Great Plains and Navision because it wanted four ERP systems—it wanted the customers. If SAP is serious about growing to 100,000 customers, why not buy 70,000 midmarket customers from Golden Gate, take advantage of the profitable maintenance stream, and then gradually migrate the base over to the All-in-One packages and Business One application?

Reforming a market

The private equity firms could easily be portrayed as a cynical bunch of financial guys who are destroying the enterprise software industry, but that wouldn't be true. The fact is this market was rotten and bloated, filled with companies in software limbo that couldn't grow, but with enough of a recurring revenue stream that they wouldn't die either. The investment bubble in the 1990s also encouraged lots of flawed business models that were unsustainable. Private equity investors are helping to reorganize the software industry and create companies that are more efficient. They have also recognized a fundamental truth that software entrepreneurs often overlook: ultimately, customers are far more valuable than code.

Innovation in the New Enterprise Application Market

Now that we understand what direction the enterprise application market is heading and what effect private equity is having on it, where does that leave innovation? As we've seen, the downside of all the venture investment is that the enterprise application software market is losing its main engine for innovation: venture-backed startups. So, as most venture capitalists lose interest in enterprise software startups, where will innovation come from? How can entrepreneurs commercialize their innovative ideas, and how can enterprise customers safely take advantage of new innovations?

Commercializing an innovative application idea requires good people, adequate funding, and willing customers. Of these, customers willing to buy, use, and help promote the new product or service are vital to creating a successful startup. Without customer traction, adequate funding and good people become nearly impossible to secure. Unfortunately for entrepreneurs, gaining traction with enterprise customers is more difficult today than at any other time since enterprise applications began to emerge in the 1980s. Customers have seen too many software companies declare bankruptcy or be acquired and eviscerated. Size is not a factor here: look at PeopleSoft, Geac, and Manugistics. This industry attrition and rapid consolidation have left customers with millions of dollars of unsupported or marginalized software, hurting the careers of many IT people along the way.

Big Four first

No wonder large organizations are leery of buying new software from any but the Big Four: Microsoft, IBM, SAP, and Oracle. While Microsoft's flirtation with buying SAP in 2003 is the exception that proves the rule, no one expects the Big Four to become the Big Three any time soon.

From an enterprise customer point of view, the Big Four are stable and have fairly comprehensive products. They have built or bought entry into most markets, with plans to expand into the important markets where they are still weak. Given the choice, most customers prefer to buy from the Big Four. When those companies are not an option for a particular area, many will wait rather than buy from a smaller vendor, making other Big Four investments while doing so.

In the late 1990s, businesses spent profligately on IT—often outside the corporate IT department—and smaller vendors prospered. Then the bubble burst, and the centralization of IT organizations and systems began a cost-cutting move that continues today and makes life harder for smaller vendors. This environment of centralized requirements and decision making favors broad, single-vendor application suites. Many companies also still need to complete the massive ERP projects they postponed in the down economy. A global rollout of ERP leaves precious little resources to take on other projects.

The Big-Four-first strategy has worked to the benefit of the Big Four and large company IT organizations. Waiting for applications minimizes business disruption, keeps IT costs down, and reduces the burden on overtaxed IT resources, but at what cost? How long can customers keep strategies at a snail's pace before the gap between business requirements and system abilities becomes unbearable?

Now IT spending is on the rise. AMR Research spending surveys find that planned IT spending has jumped to 19.5 percent in 2006—the biggest expected increase in five years. Of particular interest is 60 percent of the spending is planned for new initiatives rather than for maintaining current systems. After years of postponing investment in

IT, companies are beginning to spend to catch up to business requirements. Smaller, innovative vendors hope to benefit from this spending uptick. Things could hardly get worse for them...or could they?

The problem is much of this increased spending will go, once again, to the Big Four. Only a few companies, like aggregator Infor and some software-as-a-service (SaaS) and open source vendors, have challenged the Big Four in their traditional enterprise software categories. To make matters worse, the Big Four took advantage of the downturn and moved aggressively into nearly every other category showing growth. At current course and speed, they will capture strong market share in these new categories, as well.

Where's the exit?

Many vendor executives and their investors have been looking for a way out of this bind. Fueled by the bubble's insanely short times for companies to go from concept to successful IPO, software executives and their investors began to expect massive financial returns in less than three years. When the IPO market for software companies dried up in 2001, smaller vendors turned to exit by acquisition as their primary strategy.

Traditional venture funds are structured to realize returns within five years of their investment. Many funds actually cease operation as legal entities after 10 years. Venture firms rarely invest capital from a new fund in a company from a prior fund because investors don't want their capital bailing out underperforming investments from earlier funds. Hence, a venture investor making an investment in a company in year 3 of a fund wants to cash out within five years (year 8) and will force a sale of its shares after seven years (year 10). Given the currently anemic IPO market, selling the company is the only practical way to realize a return within that time frame.

Going public allows vendors to return capital to early investors while maintaining continuity for customers, but being acquired does not carry the same guarantee. When a smaller vendor is acquired, it often enhances the financial stability and customer service of that software company. But being acquired also often means management changes and different application directions and customer commitments, and those changes often hurt enterprise customers.

Enterprise customers need applications that will be enhanced and supported for 10 to 15 years. Given that some enterprise customers rely on vendors that have been bought and sold three or more times in the past decade, it's not surprising that some customers are looking for the exit, as well.

Toward a new software market

Customers are behaving rationally when they shy away from many venture-backed vendors. They require better alignment between their needs and the rewards for vendor executives and investors. In order to capitalize on innovative ideas, entrepreneurs and investors need to build vendors that better align with customer needs. Those that already have are the first vendors for the new software market.

In this new software market, successful smaller vendors will share the following characteristics:

- Sustainable—The half-life of a vendor cannot be shorter than the expected use of its application by a customer. Customers will not buy from companies they can't count on. New market vendor executives must have an incentive to build sustainable businesses resistant to takeovers unfriendly to customers. Startup investors need to modify their late-1990s expectations and allow companies to return capital over a longer, more realistic period of time.

- Service driven—Recurring revenue models, like those of SaaS and open source vendors, help ensure new market vendors have the steady stream of revenue to keep them sustainable and the incentive to stay customer friendly. Even acquirers must be good to customers or risk losing the recurring revenue stream they buy.

- Snap on—Enterprise customers are consolidating their infrastructure, and incompatible applications are seeing increasingly fierce resistance. New software market applications are built as composite applications, capitalizing on the platform services of the Big Four in place at the customer. They store their data in the platform application as an extension to its data structure, present themselves as an extension to its user interface, and are managed through the same utilities.

The exit-by-acquisition strategy created a fundamental misalignment between venture-backed vendors and their potential enterprise customers. This has made it harder for startup application vendors to raise capital, attract good people, and grow quickly. By taking a sustainable, service-oriented, snap-on approach, startups will see renewed interest from customers, investors, and employees. The maturing expectations of enterprise customers have created the new enterprise applications market, and innovators can be successful if they leave the dated models behind.

The Disruptive Effect
of Technology   2

The Disruptive Effect of Technology

New technologies are changing the face of business, altering how companies and their employees function. Leading the advancements is service-oriented architectures (SOAs). Vendors are touting their SOA strategies as customers try to understand how this approach will improve or affect their own architecture plans and strategies. What is clear is that SOA will transform the enterprise application market as it places new demands on the flexibility and speed required to implement and get value out of business applications. How will this transformation disrupt the market?

We explore this question by looking not only at transaction-based systems, but also at how new vehicles for collaboration can be integrated to create a whole new experience for application users. We also outline the important elements to SOA success—the ability to quickly reconfigure business processes to meet changing requirements.

This chapter also looks at other emerging technologies, including the growth of wikis and blogs, as useful business tools and the effect that the second generation of web tools, the so-called Web 2.0, is having on the greater market.

Service-Oriented Architectures: Business Needs First, Technology Second

AMR Research defines service-oriented architectures as a standards-based approach to managing services, made available by different software packages for business process orchestration, that delivers flexible reuse and reconfiguration.

Here are the key phrases:

- Standards-based—That is, agreed upon by multiple vendors in order to make software written by different organizations more interoperable. Today's SOA standards include protocols between services, data descriptions, registry definitions, display mechanisms, and orchestration rules. Services are written to common protocols that are interchangeable, unlike today's programmatic interfaces that are unique to each software application and typically vary by hardware platform, software language, and operating system.

- Services—That is, the request-response mechanism in software where one software program asks another for information. Common examples include "get customer address," "give me a credit rating for this customer," and "check the price of this item."

- Managing—The collective system of guaranteeing the security, reliability, availability, and scalability of services. This includes the creation of the service and its evolution from inception to retirement.

- Business process orchestration—One of the chief benefits of SOA is how it lets companies create new, distinguishing business processes from existing, purchased, or custom services.

- Flexible reuse and reconfiguration—Since the services are standards based, the goal is to write once, and then use it many times. This is where the biggest benefit of SOA lies, when organizations can reuse services and reconfigure business processes quickly and easily.

Service-oriented architecture is not a product to buy. Rather, it is an architectural approach to managing software designed to support the goals of the organization in a more flexible, responsive fashion. Its expected benefits of improved time to market for new business capabilities and lower cost to operate are forcing enterprise application vendors to introduce their own SOA strategies to ensure they remain a vital part of their customers' architecture. While many companies are still pondering its use, those embracing SOA see it as an opportunity for competitive advantage.

SOA in Action

An example of the value of SOAs comes from DHL.

To expand its global coverage, Deutsche Post World Net completed the acquisition of UK logistics company Exel plc in December 2005. In doing so, DHL (Deutsche Post World Net's logistics group) became the largest global provider of air freight, ocean freight, and contract logistics. Within Europe, Exel became DHL Exel Supply Chain, whereas the Exel and DHL brand names were retained separately in North America.

DHL has always specialized in providing complex supply chain management (SCM) services and logistics to large enterprise customers. Throughout the 1990s, cutting costs across their supply chain processes was DHL's and Exel's main goal. But in 2000, globalization became a much more powerful issue. At the same time, DHL acquired major new customers in the IT industry, including HP and Sun Microsystems, which needed service parts logistics support globally. The challenge it faced: how do you create such support in an environment in which IT has to integrate hundreds of disparate systems and business processes, but still offer the increased agility that customers need?

Integration complexity and business agility

By 2003, DHL Exel Supply Chain (referred to hereafter as DHL) realized that meeting customer requirements of real business agility while handling integration complexity had become so delicate that a new IT approach was essential. The best answer was SOA-based software packages. The highly flexible, component-based products promised to best respond to the agility demanded by changing business processes, organizations, and standards. Being an outsourced logistics provider, DHL has to model business processes from many different clients and many different types of businesses, and always quickly.

To appreciate the integration complexity, consider the fact that DHL's customers have hundreds of stocking locations, regional warehouses, and distribution centers. DHL has responsibility for fulfilling the functions of various parts of these supply chains. The end result could easily be that it would need to interface with the core customer business applications, including customer relationship, order management, transportation logistics, financials, enterprise resource planning (ERP), and business intelligence (BI).

Responding to the challenge

For its SOA needs, DHL turned to what it saw as a best-in-class application package as the IT backbone for its service parts logistics business. This package was developed on a multi-enterprise services architecture, which the applications have been based on since 2000.

DHL started an SOA implementation project in October 2003. It was a strategic global project from the outset, not just a tactical pilot. The project was organized into three phases: specification, development, and user acceptance testing. The project successfully went live in June 2005.

From an SOA component perspective, DHL used a mixture of the following:

- Standard off-the-shelf application components
- Extended standard vendor components
- Custom components developed by DHL

Standard components included reverse logistics, networked warehouse management, distributed order management, and inventory synchronization. These components were all deployed onto a single global production instance based on a high-availability hardware configuration.

DHL quickly discovered that the shared nature of SOA components called for a new IT organizational approach, so it formed two specialized competence center teams:

- SPL Competence Center—For business-oriented configuration and deployment of new components
- EAI Competence Center—For development and deployment of web service-based interfaces to legacy applications

The central enterprise architecture team also played a critical role in overall system design and milestone review during the implementation process.

Effect on the applications market

Oracle and SAP are both trumpeting new SOAs that will revolutionize how customers work with ERP suites. Both vendors' marketing departments have a history of getting ahead of development, leading to charges about the emperor's new clothes.

But SOA is different. In this case, the change isn't as revolutionary as the hype would indicate. Depending on a company's goals, that's not necessarily a bad thing.

For Oracle's Fusion Applications and SAP's Enterprise SOA, a few trends emerge. Neither vendor is rewriting its ERP suite according to SOA principles of componentization, reuse, and reconfiguration, as some supply chain execution and midmarket ERP vendors have done. Instead, both are wrapping the existing code base—"the blob"—exposing some services, and working on overhauling the user interface with their portal technology. Consider the following:

- SAP is apparently continuing to have separate customer, supplier, and employee masters that must be synchronized between its ERP, human resources, customer relationship management (CRM), advanced planning and scheduling (APS), and supplier relationship management (SRM) module instances. Additionally, it has an ABAP application server to keep its code alive, and its claim of 30,000 services matches the 30,000 BAPIs and iDOCs that have existed for years. Again, it appears to be wrapping existing code.

- Oracle has hundreds of services and is exposing more by making modifications to its existing PL/SQL code base or writing new ones to access the database using Java. Undocumented interfaces will still be used internally. An SOA application's services would reflect its fundamental component design and not be added on opportunistically.

Because the core code base really hasn't been opened up into separate services linked by a business process management (BPM) engine, companies may not be able to customize core business processes by modifying vendor-supplied business flows or BPEL definitions, at least for the initial release. They will be able to use BPM to link parts of their blob together or to third-party or custom applications. BPM is reduced to a coarse integration tool for extended business processes, not something to tailor the core without customizing the code. Users may be disappointed because our surveys show that reconfiguring business processes is the most anticipated benefit of SOA.

Business process rises to the top

So, what will companies do with SOA? What business opportunities does it open up, what is the fastest way to get there, and do they really have to buy into their ERP vendor's strategy?

When CIOs are asked about service-oriented architectures, the typical response is, "Why should I care?" Vague ideas of composing unique business processes aren't hitting a nerve, but fears of big, expensive upgrades are, particularly where ERP investments are concerned.

Most of the good examples of SOA are in the financial services industries, where the technique enhances reusability of code in a custom software environment. Instead, manufacturing and retail companies are implementing off-the-shelf applications, like those from SAP and Oracle. They have little interest in writing custom software and are more interested in improving their business processes.

Adoption of SOA in manufacturing and retail will lag until major enterprise vendors service-enable the bulk of their applications and put tools in the hands of business users to improve, measure performance, and prove compliance of business processes.

Consider the following reasons:

- Workflow for standardizing and accelerating business processes within the ERP suites is difficult and expensive to implement because it requires extensive programming.

- Existing ERP tools for monitoring workflow are weak, and BPM's promise of integrated performance monitoring techniques, such as activity monitoring, addresses the issue.

- Even if a company's strategy is wall-to-wall SAP or Oracle, it inevitably has some business processes that touch other applications or, more in the future, its business partner's applications. This is where composite applications will become attractive.

- Automation of extended business processes may combine automated steps, integration of several systems inside, and user interactive processes, making them a natural for BPM.

- Done right, BPM can supersede the existing inflexible workflow and give business process improvement groups better tools for continuous improvement. Now, however, the BPM abilities of the major vendors are the least mature portions of their SOA strategies.

Coordinating business process improvement, measurement, and compliance

The Sarbanes-Oxley Act (SOX) has provoked a lot of thought about how to document and test business processes to prove they are compliant. Companies are now trying to automate processes and compliance testing to reduce their ongoing costs. The management processes needed to ensure that the organization complies with the SOX controls are the same as those needed to initiate business process improvement.

Compliance and process improvement are both based on the following documented processes from which three mechanisms need to be coordinated:

- Execute process—Train employees on the process, assess their performance, and, if necessary, take steps to improve their performance and adherence to it by improving training or other actions.

- Enforce controls—Compliance adds a duty to control the process actively, perhaps by technical means, such as workflow. Companies must also audit the results to ensure that the controls work and detect any changes in the process, systems, or people that affect compliance. They must also constantly evaluate the controls to see if they are in fact meeting the desired control objectives.

- Change process—For compliance and business improvement purposes, companies need to evaluate their processes constantly and look for ways to improve them. This starts a new cycle of process design, followed by a project to implement the changed process.

A glimmer of the capability can be found in the current SOA and BPM discussions. It will take the following:

- A business process definition repository that documents the business process and drives the BPM engine—The process definition should be equally accessible to business process experts striving to improve the processes and to developers who link the definition to specific services in ERP and other applications.

- Automated performance reporting on the business process— You can't improve what you can't measure.

- Automated linkage of the process definition to training tools— Oracle showed the first hints of this by linking its iTutor training module and Internal Controls Manager.

- Automated proof of compliance and controls testing based on the business processes and controls definitions—Controls would be specified as constraints, which would detect a noncompliant business process.

Obviously, a great deal of configuration control and segregation of duties is needed here. No one person can control an entire business process, especially defining the process itself as well as the controls.

Conducting a Symphony at Owens & Minor

Business process management technologies play a pivotal role in service-oriented architectures. Services alone are like individual musicians in an orchestra without a conductor. BPM can act as a conductor, directing the tempo and orchestrating relationships between the individual services.

Owens & Minor is the nation's leading distributor of national name-brand medical/surgical supplies. It's in the business of serving hospitals and integrated healthcare systems by improving their inventory management through innovative services in supply chain management, logistics, and technology.

When Owens & Minor instituted Six Sigma process improvement initiatives to find process inefficiencies across the company, the Six Sigma executives found SOA and BPM technologies as the clear choice for implementing process improvements. Standards-based services in SOAs, along with BPM technology, were the best way to get software that wasn't written to work together to operate as one.

Two process improvement initiatives at Owens & Minor stand out:

- Customer choice—A process that compares products on customer orders with alternate products, namely ones that offer a win-win for Owens & Minor and its customer. The substitute products are less expensive for the customer and offer higher margins for the company. It sold $50 million worth of higher margin products in 2004.

- Automated debit memo—On slow-moving inventory, it needed to automate the return process while adhering to the manufacturer's return policies. It used BPM to validate existing rules and manage the return process, including collaboration with the suppliers. It expects $1 million in savings per year.

Service creation is still a very frustrating process; Owens & Minor uses a 25-year-old ERP system. The hardest part of the SOA development included the seven person-months of development and design of the initial service, and another seven person-months of testing. Success stories like Owens & Minor are more often found in those companies that first adopt methodologies like Six Sigma, and then select technologies to implement their process improvements. Selection criteria includes sophisticated development capabilities coupled with user-friendly process design and change management capabilities.

Choices, choices—if you are looking for distinct business processes

There are three major choices companies can make as they eye the SOA opportunity:

- Ignore it—Accept that ERP, as it works today, is doing what it needs to do. The focus should be on getting more value out of the present abilities and upgrade only when more functionality is needed.

- Buy in—Companies commit to the ERP vendor's SOA framework for the long haul. They start phasing out third-party portals, enterprise application integration tools, and development tools in favor of the ERP vendors. Don't get too excited, though: the worst thing a company can do is get ahead of its ERP vendor's functionality and end up compromising goals, then have to redevelop the extended application. Remember that there are risks in taking the first release of an ERP vendor's new modules.

- Branch out—If the ERP vendor is only part of the IT environment and a company already has another SOA vendor's tools deployed, it should consider using those tools for its SOA vision. The existing and future exposed services of the ERP vendor will be useful, and the company can start today—without waiting for the ERP vendor's SOA version in 2008. Aren't standards wonderful?

Most companies are still trying to figure out what the most advantageous approach would be. All SOA framework vendors need to get more specific about use cases for service-oriented architectures, since buyers are still struggling to envision how they would use them.

The good news: the risk is low and companies have time. Long term, becoming more "SOA-like" is a good thing for ERP suites, and this approach is far less risky than rewriting the entire application as an SOA-based system. As companies understand this, they usually breathe a sigh of relief and start thinking harder about when exactly they have to upgrade.

A few recommendations:

- Understand the limits to business process reconfiguration of core processes. This is a long-haul technology, and vendors will be modifying their products for months and years.

- Line up use cases for service-oriented architectures now. What business processes should be automated, mistake-proof, measured, and extended to business partners?

- For any extensive deployment of a more general-purpose SOA framework product, perhaps used to develop customer-facing websites and applications, evaluate its abilities. There will inevitably be some coexistence with the ERP vendor's framework, but it may be possible to accelerate the SOA project with a more mature product and existing in-house expertise.

The midmarket gold mine

A lot of SOA talk concerns which industries are embracing it first—such as financial services and telecommunications—and how it will affect large enterprises. Often overlooked is the opportunity for SOA in the midmarket, where companies often trail large enterprises when it comes to technology. SOA might just level the playing field, making it quicker and less expensive for small and midsize businesses (SMBs) to assemble and maintain innovative software that provides competitive advantage.

Several factors play into the opportunity for SOA in these smaller companies and divisions or subsidiaries of larger companies:

- New leadership—Many smaller companies are family-run businesses. As a new generation moves into leadership roles, they bring new expectations about the benefits of technology and how it can be used to grow the business profitably. These new leaders are likely to be more willing to embrace new technology.

- SOA-ready packaged applications—Several of the midmarket ERP vendors, most recently Epicor and Syspro, report they have made the transition to service-oriented architectures. Many of these packaged apps are built on top of Microsoft's .NET framework or Progress Software's OpenEdge platform. Both companies have been at the forefront of distributed computing and SOA.

- Extensibility—This new class of SOA-based packaged applications makes it easier for companies to extend the products with minimal staff effort—a significant requirement for small and midsize businesses. For example, one Syspro customer has extended its products to build a warehouse management system with just one full-time programmer.

The opportunity for service-oriented architectures in the midmarket has not gone unnoticed by the major vendors either. Major application and infrastructure vendors have already developed or tailored existing products to target the midmarket. Whether they will be able to go downmarket successfully remains to be seen, but it presents the biggest growth market for these big vendors that already have the lion's share of the large enterprise.

The adoption of SOA by smaller companies may also turn out to be good for large enterprises, as well. They will now have a more cost-effective means of working with smaller customers and suppliers. In fact, a likely initial use of service-oriented architectures among large enterprises will be extending external-facing applications to smaller partners, which may now have an SOA-based means of collaborating. When speaking about the benefits of SOA, proponents always focus on agility and reuse. These are the most obvious, but the potential network effect of companies of all sizes embracing SOA may be the biggest benefit of all.

Wikis and Blogs: New Collaboration Tools Force Change

While much of the focus on service-oriented architecture has been on transaction-oriented systems, the next generation of composite applications will be a seamless blending of transaction and collaboration, supporting structured and unstructured information. Putting technology that is easier to use and more powerful in the hands of users is the main goal, and that requires the consolidation of traditional enterprise applications and new collaborative technologies, such as wikis and blogs.

Wikis and blogs may seem hokey and faddish to some, but they're likely the next big factor in knowledge management for enterprises. They'll play increasingly vital roles in helping companies capture, retain, and transfer crucial business knowledge, improve customer service, manage and communicate change, and generally mitigate the pain and cost of lost expertise. With the retirement of hordes of baby boomers looming, enterprises better pay attention.

Defining and positioning blogs and wikis for the enterprise is difficult. While they've quickly garnered momentum in public domains, they're only just emerging in the enterprise. And in both cases, since their nature is to respond, adapt to, and promote change, defining them and their appropriate roles is like trying to nail Jell-O to a wall.

First the discussion must be separated into what they are from a technology perspective versus what they are as a mode or genre of knowledge sharing and collaboration. The latter, if you really want them to work, is a far more important distinction. While wikis and blogs have distinct definitions and uses, they share a theme: make information capture, transfer, and dissemination easier and more accessible for the everyday Internet citizen—that is, the enterprise employee, partner, customer, et al.

Blogs and Wikis 101

Blog

"Blog" is simply short for web log, with its implication as an online journal. Blogs focus on one person, with an emphasis on the person's authority and expertise on a topic. Other authors may respond via feedback, provoking further discussion. Blogs are often addressed to internal audiences, such as a CEO communicating strategy to company employees or investors. Enterprises are also beginning to use customer-facing blogs to publish views and gather feedback.

Wiki

"Wiki" comes from a Hawaiian word for "fast" or "quick." Wikis employ many, often anonymous, contributors and editors. While the archetype for wikis is the well-known Wikipedia, most enterprises are starting to roll out wikis for internal use, often to allow dynamic authoring, contribution, and access to process and change management information.

How they fit: a knowledge management paradox

The idea of more tools for knowledge management creates a paradox for companies that have long strived to create a single place, typically a portal and/or a content management system, where workers go to share and access information. Effective knowledge management strategies tend to urge employees toward these single environments, and it's not entirely clear yet how blogs and wikis will work with them rather than competing for people's attention and contribution. It is clear that they should and must work together eventually. But we're talking about an immature market with few proven examples or best practices and a marketplace of more than 80 products, with the big vendors only making vague promises of capabilities down the line.

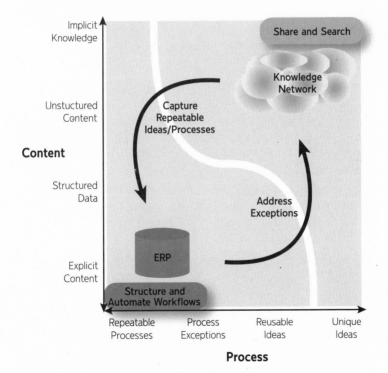

Figure 1: The AMR Research Knowledge and Innovation Swerve

Unfortunately, all this flux paralyzes far too many companies, as does the continual debate over new technology, often under the guise of "governance." The need to create a culture of contribution, with a view toward capturing innovation, retaining vital company knowledge and intellectual property, and improving consistency of customer service, may far outweigh concerns over any deep integration with existing systems today.

And companies must recognize, accommodate, and appreciate the innovation, creativity, and people-power that really drives a company's success. Most out-of-the-box thinking defies systematic capture and categorization. Any effort to cram it into an ERP system is futile and fruitless.

As one early adopter at a large grocer revealed, wikis and blogs, social networks, and other publicly available, innovative modes of collaboration and communication are on their way. Ignore them at your peril, and use them to your success. Sure, the aging workforce may be unaware or resistant, but the new generation has grown up using them, and they are bringing their habits and expertise along.

Using wikis and blogs in the enterprise

Wiki and blog use is already widespread in large companies, though businesses rarely have a thoroughly refined plan for them. Several members of a CIO panel at AMR Research's Strategy 21 Conference in January 2006 mentioned prominent plans to use wikis to support a range of new business initiatives. In fact, having questioned many of our clients on the topic, companies that don't employ wikis or blogs, whether the CIO knows about them or not, are quickly becoming a rarity.

IT organizations and enterprises that aren't actively using wikis and blogs must soon face their existence. They're quickly becoming as undeniable as instant messaging (IM), e-mail, and Internet access itself were not so long ago. Whether wanted or not, new employees are bringing them along into companies with the skills to use them. In the meantime, businesses will also have to deal with the existence of external public blogs and wikis and the risks and opportunities that they bring.

Gathered from interviews with customers and software providers, what follows are a few ideas and examples of how to put wikis and blogs to good business use.

IT change management, project tracking, and documentation

Much of the early enterprise use of wikis and blogs was to help IT departments manage document change. As they work more actively with partners, supporting employees in various locations and in multiple time zones, they needed a persistent way to see what changes were made and why.

IT is the audience. For starters, IT departments are pressured by a shift toward service-oriented architectures and thus in dire need. Secondly, with the expectation that their businesses will inevitably use them, they're learning about wiki and blog technology, as well as the resources required to manage them, and evaluating the ideal use cases for the business.

Executive alignment and corporate communications

Companies are also using wikis and blogs for corporate communications, often allowing executives to convey and share their ideas with employees, board members, investors, and customers. In general, the goal is to help unify the business and align resources toward accomplishing enterprise goals. This is especially effective when bringing merging business entities together.

The use of blogs and wikis is far better than the typical, one-way "message from the CEO" newsletter. Instead, innovative executives use blogs to generate discussion among employees, gather feedback, and collect alternative points of view. This tends to interest and engage employees far more than a pushed message, and it gives the community a sense that it influences the company's strategic direction.

Better yet, the community's impression of influence is not mistaken. Executives come to understand the employee response to the stated strategy. They can adopt useful ideas and modify that strategy (that is, they innovate). One company we talked with intends to publish the CEO's strategy as a wiki and—believe it or not—allow employees to edit and alter the document freely. Risky and provocative, no doubt, but it's sure to get more attention and have the potential for more value than a newsletter.

Customer service and self-service

Blog and wiki use is already widespread for customer service and self-service. Call center reps are finding that wikis, as dynamic self-structuring documents, offer a more updated, cohesive knowledge base from which to address customer problems. In some cases, customer service organizations are extending wiki-style knowledge bases to their customers, allowing them to add to it for the benefit of the broader community. Some wiki tools can also be personalized and secured to show customer service representatives an insider's view of the same documents the customer sees.

Blogs, wikis, and similar mechanisms are also being used by retailers on customer-facing sites. Amazon.com uses blogs, wikis, plogs (personal web logs), and social tagging to generate site stickiness and direct customers toward desired products. Blogs are often published by book authors, and wikis are used to allow customers to enhance information about products.

Putting the Tech in High-Tech

One of the world's largest high-tech manufacturers views wikis and blogs as part of its overarching knowledge management strategy, helping to promote adoption of its existing technology investments.

Rather than an alternative to more traditional systems, wikis are part of its content management and collaboration platform. With 64,000 users in 320 locations in 73 countries, and in a business that thrives on getting ideas to market before the competition, the company cares about innovation.

Supplier and partner collaboration

Wikis are also proving to be valuable assets for companies actively working with external partners to create, develop, and introduce new products. Keeping track of product specifications and documentation through lengthy product lifecycles has long been a bugbear for engineers, as has handing off cumbersome and error-prone product information to marketing and support groups when the same specialized applications are shared.

The process becomes exponentially more difficult with manufacturers looking to external partners and contractors for joint development. Living documents like wikis are a means to maintain continuity and consistency among disparate groups using various applications.

Employee learning and human capital management

Companies are using collaborative web technologies to help alleviate the cost of lost expertise while cutting down training time and reducing startup costs for new hires. Knowledge workers are often more amenable to contributing to wikis and blogs, with their accessibility and emphasis on supporting the community and peers, than they are to entering information into hungry, selfish structured systems.

On the opposite end, companies are using wikis to convey knowledge to new hires. This can be highly sophisticated and specialized information, such as that contributed by engineers, or it can be simple things like company glossaries, HR process instructions and forms, and employee directories to help workers get up to speed quickly.

Web 2.0

Not so long ago, companies around the world flung open their traditional IT budgets to take advantage of the burgeoning web. This money, as many of us have direct experience with, was not always well spent.

So along comes Web 2.0, and companies, jaded with the experience of the last several years, are understandably suspicious about the hype and skeptical about the impact to their business. There's no question, though, that change has been happening under our noses. Businesses have to find fruitful ways to take advantage.

What is Web 2.0?

Web 2.0 is an advancement of our understanding and use of the web as a communication and collaboration medium for business and personal use. It's characterized by active end-user and community participation, and supported by technology equipped to support many modes of integration and interaction.

We're reluctant to give the term Web 2.0 an enthusiastic blessing. Certainly it's caught the attention of the press, the subtle joke appealing to IT pros and business people alike, and it's quickly become a buzz term for vendors to glom onto and exploit. Of course,

Web 2.0 is no clear-cut upgrade: it doesn't come on a CD, and you can't download it. Plus, no patches will get you from version 1.0 to 2.0 (not that there really is a Web 1.0, anyway).

On the other hand, we'll agree that the web has reached a second phase in the sense of being used for purposes for which it's uniquely suited, rather than only being used to replace existing technology, like traditional publishing, paper, telephone, electronic data interchange (EDI), and the like. For example, social networking as we've come to know it on the web simply wasn't feasible with traditional media or communications mechanisms. Phase 2 is where we exploit the web for what it's uniquely equipped: not simply to emulate, replace, and streamline existing processes, but to create new ones entirely.

The evolving frontier

Web 2.0's advancement is really a maturing of our understanding and use of the web as a medium for communication and collaboration. While various technological advances make the web more capable and versatile in serving more advanced purposes, the primary forces driving Web 2.0 come from business, community, government, and, most prominently now, consumer demand.

Much of the Web 2.0 hype thus far has promoted an endless, confusing array of new technologies, tools, and applications that enable or exploit the evolving web. Keeping in mind that demand ultimately translates into technology success, and with too much technology still out there looking for problems to solve, Web 2.0 is a frontier where products, services, and standards battle for recognition and adoption. It is where they'll ultimately combine into broader categories for strength, or where they'll wither and die altogether.

That said, the governing principle involves addressing the faults of the earlier web in its lack of appeal, accessibility, and utility for the end user and the community. Besides wikis and blogs, there are other technology developments to watch:

- The semantic web—This is probably the most fundamental piece of the evolving web. Based on using richer, standardized metadata and a universal ontology known as the resource description framework (RDF), it's a logical extension of HTML and XML that aspires to provide a universal language for human and machine processing of web information.

- Rich client support—Including AJAX, Microsoft's Atlas, and Adobe's Flex, client support efforts are all geared toward providing more appealing, useful, and productive environments for end users, whether accessed through web browsers, cell phones, kiosks, or televisions.

- Media and communications convergence—The ability to use the web as a universal channel for computing, rich media, and communications is a long anticipated development for businesses and home users alike. Technology is no longer holding us back. Rather, the maneuverings and manipulations of the oft-competing providers are the primary forces of resistance. Still, home users, having already availed themselves of services like Vonage and Skype, are pressuring businesses to move forward.

- Navigation, search, and retrieval (NSR)—Search has had to evolve in step with the evolving web. Search engines like Google and Yahoo!, rather than specific sites or applications, are becoming the de facto launching points for people seeking information on the public world wide web. This search-as-interface demand has found its way into business, where information is strewn among a limitless variety of often hard-to-access systems, forms, formats, and locations. It only seems to be getting worse.

- Web data mining and analytics—Of course, analytics and business intelligence are far from new, but with more active participation on the web among end users and communities, they must be applied to less structured information to help companies recognize market opportunities and mitigate risk.

- Social networking techniques—Methods such as expertise identification and social tagging are increasingly being applied to worker productivity, human resource allocation, and retention and reuse of enterprise knowledge assets.

So, what should companies do about Web 2.0? First, be neither blinded by the hype nor blindsided by the opportunity that the evolving web may present to a business. Regard it as an integral factor, and not something entirely new and divorced from current business goals, initiatives, and systems.

Consider the impact of the evolving web on key business and IT initiatives:

- Service-oriented architecture—The same foundation that will allow companies to consume and convey web services as means of intra- and intercompany integration and collaboration is the one intended to support the evolving world wide web.

- Software as a service—The same end-user and community appeal and accessibility that's helped garner loyalty on the evolving web has helped drive the success of salesforce.com and other newer technology providers. The enhancement and extensions of such services also could well resemble evolving web techniques like social networks and wikis.

- Demand-driven supply networks—The web is becoming a much richer source of demand information, and therefore a much more versatile and efficient mechanism through which to sense and respond to demand.

Prepared companies will tune into the useful information that lies outside of a their data stores. They will also employ technologies like search and text analytics to put user- and community-generated information into a business context, aiding decision-making rather than causing distraction, interruption, or information overload.

Web 3.0?

Wondering what Web 3.0 will be or when it's coming? Theoretically, Phase 3 is when the technology becomes universally understood and adopted for like purposes by all its users. The effect is that it works its way into the fabric not only of our IT systems, but of our society. Users take it for granted because it's reliable and offers so little competitive distinction that it rarely warrants attention.

In other words, don't hold your breath for the beta release.

The New Role of Portals

When companies use portal products to pursue long-term, strategic initiatives, they ignore the future of portals at their peril. Businesses are pulling together the information, processes, and people required to address compliance. They're also using portals to engage and retain customers, building dashboards to sense and respond to industry changes as they occur, and establishing and maintaining vital connections with suppliers and partners. So, they probably won't want to rewrite it all for the sake of the latest gadget. With some foresight, though, they'll mitigate this risk.

One way to do that is to ensure portal frameworks employ a service-oriented architecture. In fact, portal efforts have already proven to be a prime mover of SOA. While IT organizations have found technology-driven pursuits like SOA difficult to justify across the enterprise, they've found specific portal projects easy—especially where no packaged application exists or provides sufficient differentiation.

Enterprise portals must employ an architecture that supports a company's changing needs. In fact, the portal is exactly that for many of the enterprise portal framework vendors, which now constitute the largest software vendors in the world.

It's true: Microsoft, IBM, SAP, Oracle, and BEA are not only the presidents in the portal market, they're also clients. However, it goes further than that. Vendors are using the portal as a vehicle to move their customers forward and insulate them from the pain of their own transformations as they shift to SOAs, seek to integrate their own mounting acquisitions, and respond to changes in the way customers buy and deploy their software.

The portal as competitive battlefront

When the notion of the portal was introduced a decade ago, it threatened lots of established enterprise vendors. Many have tried to turn this into an opportunity, either by jumping wholly on board the portal, attempting to alter its course, or finding a way to sink it.

Still, with so much consolidation in the general enterprise IT market, large vendors can only grow by invading each others' territories. As much as any space at the crux of infrastructure and application, enterprise, and desktop, the portal market embodies the battlefield for the enterprise software market (see Figure 2).

Understanding the vendors' stakes, intentions, and angles of attack is of supreme importance when devising a portal strategy. Customers must ensure their providers' motivations line up with their own and that established providers work well together.

The disappearance of the pure-play portal vendors, with BEA's acquisition of Plumtree, means no vendor regards the portal as its primary product focus. Rather, vendors often use the portal to advance or protect their traditional, more lucrative sources of business. This, too, often compromises their willingness or ability to integrate with systems from other vendors. It also means the demise of portal purity, which forces us to reconsider what constitutes independence, or application and infrastructure agnosticism. It also forces us to consider whether striving for such architectural principles is even worthwhile.

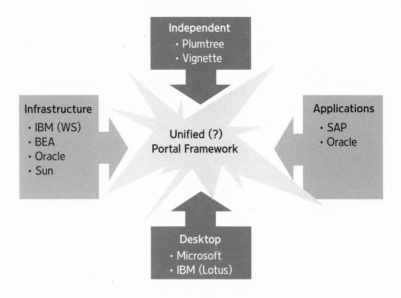

Figure 2: Vendors clash, customers clash

Customers want portal frameworks to bring information and applications together into cohesive, efficient environments so that IT, business, and end users can securely share information, collaborate, and coordinate a range of efforts to accomplish business goals. They want the portal to reduce the pain of conflict between competing vendors. In too many cases, the vendors are perpetuating the problem.

The unbound portal

The notion of the portal will soon move from something tangible and demonstrable, in the form of a website, to an abstract point of access and presence: the unbound portal. This is why AMR Research has always resisted defining the portal as others have: as a browser-based interface. Surely the portal will continue to act as a secure, single point of access for individuals to companies, and vice versa. It will also employ broader web-based technologies, including web services, to serve its purposes. It won't, however, necessarily be embodied in a web browser.

Rather, in the not very distant future, the portal will act as a virtual point of presence, accessible from whatever interface, system, device, or application happens to sit in front of the end user.

In part, it's the technical limitations of browsers that lead us to this conclusion: clients need richer, higher performing interfaces, and though emerging techniques and standards show some promise, they are continually moving targets. Witness the fairly well-established and adopted portal standards, like JSR 168, and their inability, at least anytime soon, to accommodate quickly emerging interface features and techniques.

There's still no easy way to ensure portal compatibility or adaptability to a wide and growing variety of devices—not just dedicated computing devices, but iPods, home entertainment hubs, store kiosks, and cars—without a lot of transformation and testing. We've got to find common denominators that work for the long term.

This is not to say that the portal won't continue to offer a user interface. It just won't displace user interfaces that people are already accustomed to using. Through the unbound portal, office workers will employ web services and participate in business processes without ever consciously visiting a website.

We're already beginning to see the enterprise portal concept turned around. That is, the unbound portal is not only an end user's doorway to the enterprise, but increasingly the enterprise's doorway, and an enormous range of other constituencies' doorways, to the end user.

As a virtual point of presence, the portal will become the point where people deal with the increasing demands on their time and the disruption that a continual barrage of information and communication brings them in their personal, family, community, and work environments.

Relief will come in the form of the unbound portal, which entails three common denominators: identity, presence, and convergence (see Figure 3).

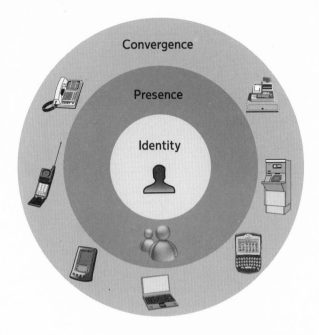

Figure 3: The unbound portal

Identity

The unbound portal will require a more authoritative, consistent, complete, reusable, and especially secure notion of identity.

A single point of access, whether it's the individual to the company or the company to the individual, is downright scary from a security and privacy perspective. But identity isn't entirely about risk. For example, companies are using core structured data about employees, mapping it to certifications and expertise, and often associating it with unstructured content they produce in order to create knowledge networks, with a view toward capturing innovation and alleviating the pain of lost expertise.

Presence

You may know presence as the symbol that shows your availability in an IM client. Here, you let coworkers and friends know when you're busy or away from your desk. You may have already noticed the symbol, in the same state, beside contact names in your e-mail client, and maybe even in your office productivity and enterprise applications. But soon a more sophisticated and pervasive presence will allow you to manage other organizations' and individuals' access to you: by constituency, communication channel, application, and location.

Convergence

The third pillar must be the realization of convergence: the ability for us to access all our communication and collaboration in one place.

The technology limitations are not the obstacles they once were. Consumers and companies are beginning to prove the value of collaboration platforms, including asynchronous and real-time messaging and voice over Internet protocol (VoIP). Business issues involving compliance and improving customer service are tipping the cost/benefit scales, even considering the effort to implement the technology and change corporate behavior.

Companies must begin to regard web services as more than just a mechanism for system-to-system integration. Rather, web services, invoked on the unbound portal, must become appealing and accessible to end users and consumers. Consider what opportunities or risks will arise when consumers can simply invoke your business services by selecting portlets on their personal portal. You may soon be competing on an entirely different playing field.

Planning for SOA
and the New World of
Composite Applications   3

Planning for SOA and the New World of Composite Applications

While the previous chapter looked at the disruptive effect that service-oriented architectures (SOAs) and other technologies will have on the enterprise application marketplace, this chapter focuses more on the changes to people, process, and technology that companies must make to get the most out of SOAs. It also looks at what companies need to tackle when planning for this new reality and giving organizations the flexibility and speed to gain the benefits that SOAs promise.

Overcoming the Hurdles

A faster and more flexible reconfiguration of business processes is the No. 1 reason companies gave for deploying a SOA in an AMR Research survey conducted at the end of 2005 (see Figure 1).

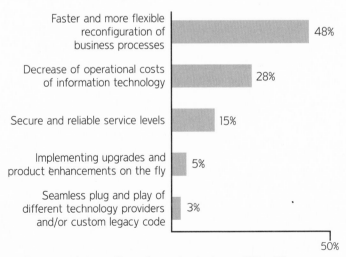

Base: Companies that are either using or planning to use SOA, n=99

Figure 1: Expected benefits of SOA

Many successful SOA implementations have met this objective, but had to conquer the following problems first:

- Governance, or when to "leave and layer" versus "rip and replace"—While SOA promises unprecedented software interoperability, it also will challenge the very nature of governance: IT teamwork and interorganizational communication. If your IT organization was not tuned into the needs of the business before service-oriented architecture, SOA implementations will magnify that deficiency. IT shops can easily become enamored with the promises of SOA and jump head first into the technologies without recognizing what is truly missing from their organization: teamwork, collaboration, project prioritization, and business justification.

- New development model—Companies must develop services for widespread reuse with well-defined interfaces and a repository for documentation. While documentation has usually been an afterthought in most software development projects, it comes up front with SOA. In fact, the very nature of SOA suggests a radical departure from the traditional software development model (design, develop, deploy, manage) in which the development was performed by a core group of developers all working on the same platform. Now development forces IT professionals to become better collaborators when developing SOA-based technology. Services that must be knit together from various sources will require an unprecedented focus on collaboration for success.

- Service policy management—New types of questions arise from services that can be used in new ways by many types of consumers. What is the process of developing a service? Where should those services reside? How should a service be described for maximum reuse? When changes are made, how should they be tested? Who defines and modifies services? Who is allowed access to the services? What quality of service must be provided? Who will pay for building the service? Who will pay for service infrastructure? How will the interdependencies of services be managed? How do we expose services to outside parties? Success with SOA requires answers to these questions.

- Security—An environment for managing the identity of consumers and services is mandatory in SOA. While most companies have an identity management policy in place for human users, services themselves become a new type of user and consumer in SOA, exceeding the limits of most identity management systems in production today. This issue has limited many companies from exposing services to customers and suppliers and is the primary reason for most SOA initiatives being kept to internal use in a controlled environment.

- Data transformation—Using commonly accepted industry-standard interfaces between systems does not eradicate the problem of data transformation. Because the underlying systems have been developed independently, the ongoing problem of matching the contextual meaning of data found in separate systems remains, and will stymie even the most astute data architects.

- Service repositories—Every company providing SOA middleware infrastructure is offering its own version of a service repository. The service repository contains the services and the necessary artifacts that describe that service to the world. The problem? Today's service repositories are all proprietary and create the potential for vendor lock-in. While each vendor promises that it is working with the WS* standards and will readily adopt the industry standard when it becomes available, each also has a unique proprietary view of the situation. Global multinational corporations will likely have multiple service repositories, creating a new and different hurdle to integration: service repository integration.

WS*: W3C Bringing Standards to Services

The organization that brought you the World Wide Web, the W3C, has been working for many years on developing web services standards, the WS in WS*. Under the advisory committee, the W3C Web Services Activity, the organization is designing the infrastructure, defining the architecture, and creating the core technologies for web services. As part of that effort, the group developed the simple object access protocol (SOAP) 1.2 XML-based messaging framework, which the W3C released for recommendation in June 2003, and the SOAP Message Transmission Optimization Mechanism (MTOM), recommended in January 2005. Current work includes publishing a web services description language (WSDL) primer and specifications, as well as WSDL resource description language (RDL) mapping and implementations. More specifications and recommendations are expected in the months to come as the group tries to standardize how web services are used to make them easier for all.

Addressing these issues will be vital for SOA success. SOA will expose the gap between the disciplined and undisciplined IT organization, creating the opportunity for fantastic success and spectacular failure. These hurdles fall into three primary categories—governance and people, process, and technology and IT governance—into which we will dive next. Success with SOA will hinge on your organization's ability to coordinate the three categories to meet changing business requirements.

The Governance and People Hurdle

Much of the service-oriented architecture talk today is about the technologies that companies will adopt to deliver it: business process management (BPM), enterprise service bus (ESB), and service registries and repositories, just to name a few. However, when we speak to vendors and user companies that are adopting SOA, it is immediately clear that success is predicated on the company's ability to morph its processes, culture, and organization to deliver a more flexible, component-based architecture.

Don't underestimate this change. It is one of the most significant cultural changes to hit the IT organization in the past 20 years.

Core competencies for success

In the traditional model for software development, developers have ownership of an application, or a complete segment of an application, and are responsible for developing every aspect of it. The applications that get created are designed to solve a specific business problem, often without regard to how this application needs to interact with others. These monolithic applications often recreate the business logic that exists within other applications.

The new model calls for building component parts designed for reuse and assembly of new composite applications based on a mix of existing and new services. It creates an environment in which developers are more dependent on one another to ensure that the services being created will interoperate with existing services or ones yet to be built. As such, it places a premium on the core competencies an IT organization must have to be successful:

- Portfolio management—Portfolio management in an SOA model has two aspects. The first is as a mechanism for evaluating and prioritizing which services or composite applications should get funded. This is designed to foster alignment and maximize return on investment. The second aspect is portfolio management for existing applications and services to continually evaluate where investment should continue based on factors such as cost, utilization, strategic fit, and quality/performance.

- Architecture review board (ARB)—The whole area of enterprise architecture will require a face lift for many organizations. The ARB is responsible for defining SOA standards and ensuring that people are using existing services to get the reuse benefit that SOA promises. They also play a critical role in the portfolio management discussion.

- Iterative development—Companies that have successfully embraced SOA have often changed the core process for how the work gets done. Agile development methodologies are common. This new process can deliver new capabilities quickly, ones that closely match end-user requirements.

- New testing requirements—Many testing tools and practices are designed with the monolithic application in mind. A new approach to testing, as well as updates to testing tools, will likely be necessary.

- Aligned incentives—Perhaps the most important of all changes will be to the goals and objectives of developers. The incentives should be closely mapped to the goals and objectives of the overall strategy for SOA. This should help guide the desirable behaviors to ensure success.

One of the most common IT governance inquiries is about how to start shifting mindsets toward IT's value and away from its costs. The role technology plays in helping people be innovative is a major element of that discussion. Examples include developing software that lets salespeople identify their most profitable customers, or an automated portal that slashes the time it takes to bring new suppliers online. IT does play a role in automating innovative business processes, and the technology to do that is now largely based on service-oriented architectures.

Enormous impact

The evolution to SOA will create necessary change in the current operating model for many IT organizations—ones that are not structured to support this more fluid model. The impact will be particularly striking across the following areas of IT governance:

- Investment planning—The current model for evaluating potential investments is usually split into two processes: one for big new investments, and one for smaller ongoing requirements. SOA's compartmentalized development model essentially combines those two notions—where nothing is ever 100 percent new, but rather assembled from existing and new. This will force a change in how we build the business case for these investments, how we prioritize, and how we measure benefits, since most current portfolio management processes are designed to support long-term projects and will not support the higher volumes of investment candidates.

- Software development—Traditional software developers are like artisans, carefully building all of the pieces of a product so that they fit well together. SOA development is more like an assembly line, where putting together standard components to create new things is the primary focus. SOA will essentially put the artisans on the assembly line, working on discrete services and assembling them with existing internal services or even third-party services. Testing models will also need to change to support distributed composite applications that may span multiple companies' service repositories.

- Change management—SOA will create an environment in which change is more dynamic, since you can update one part of the composite application without breaking the whole. Better automation and control of the change process as well as new standards for version control are necessary.

- Maintenance and operations—SOA will change the way we manage our applications. It's relatively easy to monitor an application when it is well contained within a known set of infrastructure. A composite application will potentially be distributed across the infrastructure and even outside the firewall where companies have little or no control on the performance characteristics of a service.

- Security—A new model for application security will be required, as well—one that respects the security inherent in the existing applications that are exposing services, as well as a layer that maintains that integrity across the composite application.

Act now

So yes, SOA is going to affect almost all aspects of IT. While this much change is daunting, there are steps that can be taken ahead of SOA adoption that will make this transition easier:

- Improve processes—Evaluate the maturity of important processes that span the IT organization, like change management, resource management, and incident management. Companies are investigating best practice frameworks, like the IT infrastructure library (ITIL), to give them a consistent process definition and language to improve the effectiveness of these core processes.

- Improve demand and portfolio management—The imbalance between demand and supply in IT will always be an issue, and SOA is only going to make it worse by increasing end-user expectations regarding speed to delivery. One of the best ways to deal with this is to put a process to better manage demand. Learning to say no to things based on real business information may be the most important competency a service-centric IT organization can have.

- Clearly define an enterprise architecture—The last wave of computing change, from client/server to Internet, threw the discipline of enterprise architecture out the window to focus on the promise of Internet computing. This left many IT organizations with expensive applications sitting on the shelf, or applications that don't interoperate well because of lack of a broader architecture vision. Today's companies can't make the same mistake. A strong architecture will help ensure the agility that SOA promises can be maintained while adapting to meet changing business requirements.

- Use business service management—Customers are increasingly thinking in terms of business processes or services. If IT infrastructure is managed in terms of servers and routers, performance won't be related to how a company's customer views the world. Start defining and managing the main services IT provides, and measure IT performance in the context of those services.

The Process Hurdle

SOA deployments are mostly internal, AMR Research surveys have found. Early adopters have deployed the technologies in safe, controlled environments, often embarking on pilots where most of the collaboration is with employees or software applications managed by a single department or company.

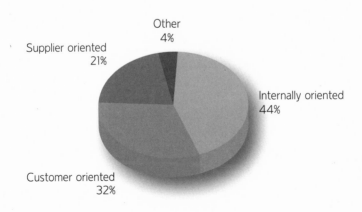

Base: Companies currently using SOA, n=28

Figure 2: Focus of SOA deployment today

For these internal SOA deployments, the survey showed the main investment was in application integration, followed by IT help desk request and response activities and employee on-boarding (see Figure 3). Each of these represents environments that are relatively stable and where the IT staff can control variables such as service users, protocols, and security. It's just a safe bet for first-time implementers.

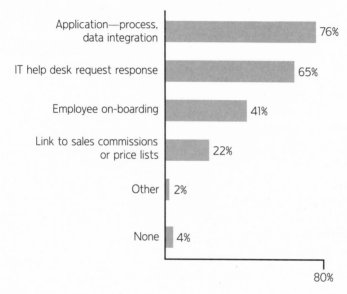

Base: Companies that are either using or planning to use SOA, n=99

Figure 3: SOA deployments—internal

But in the future, surveyed companies plan a substantial rise in SOA deployments that touch their customers. This is a strong sign for SOA in general because the early adopters have become comfortable with the technologies and are willing to use them for processes that support customer interaction (see Figure 4).

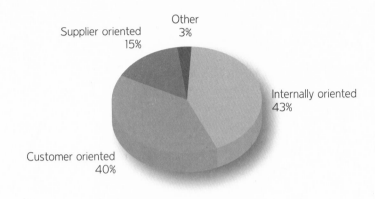

Supplier oriented
15%

Other
3%

Internally oriented
43%

Customer oriented
40%

Base: Companies currently using SOA, n=99

Figure 4: Focus of SOA deployments in future

At these advanced SOA companies, e-commerce website enhancement is the main investment, by almost a two-to-one margin. The reason: IT professionals can write one service and use it multiple times.

For example, a "check inventory" service can be written and used for custom point-of-sale systems, handheld warehouse devices, customer service return systems, and the e-commerce self-service customer portal. Using service-oriented techniques reduces the cost of maintenance of the check inventory service, since a single source of software performs that task regardless of the requesting software.

Some companies are also looking to SOAs to better collaborate with suppliers. For these companies, the leading investments are supplier performance portals and vendor-managed inventory (VMI) systems (see Figure 5).

Customer

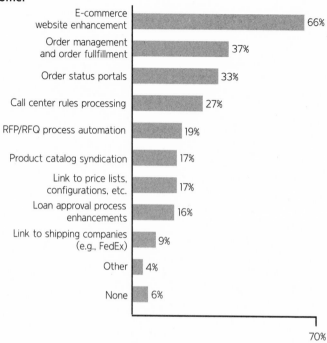

Supplier

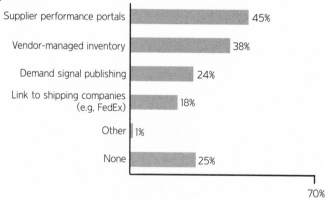

Base: Companies that are either using or planning to use SOA, n=99

Figure 5: SOA deployments—customer and supplier

SOA in warehousing

SOA has already proven itself in the warehouse management system (WMS) market. For several years, many of the leading vendors have completely restructured their applications into libraries of small functional components, allowing the application flow itself to be constructed from a configurable business process workflow. This use of SOA proves its value by allowing customization and innovation to coexist with upgradeable vendor-released software. It also allows the rapid reconfiguring of business processes.

WMS implementations have traditionally required high levels of customization compared to other supply chain management (SCM) applications. Highly customized systems are rarely upgraded because the cost and time is prohibitive. SOA provides a way for customizations, which in many cases represent innovative processes, to coexist nonintrusively with vendor-released software. Because of this, customers can regularly take on upgrades without the high cost of retrofitting.

One sporting goods retailer reports it has a special process whereby it customizes a cross-dock flow from receiving process to one preparing for store delivery in its distribution center. This custom process, not available in the WMS, was added to the system workflow. Even though the system is made up of approximately 20 percent custom process, the retailer was regularly able to take and process upgrades from the vendor.

One of the reasons WMS applications are heavily customized is that customer requirements tend to fall on the fulfillment process. Special processing requests by certain customers for certain products often wil! sacrifice productivity in the distribution center if they're not able to be automated and integrated into the regular fulfillment process. Integrating these custom, highly changing requirements is costly in traditional systems, so in many cases they become workarounds to current processes.

One third-party logistics (3PL) company says the flexibility to reconfigure application flow via the business process workflow in its warehouse management system (built using SOA) was instrumental in it being able to win and retain new outsourcing business. Its speed to bring up a new client—whose processes are always different than any other client—increased to within one to two months from four to eight months with its old systems.

To get the full value of SOA, however, these customers say it is important to invest in learning the vendor's workflow configurator tools to make the most use out of the flexible customization. Also, SOA in and of itself isn't a solution for problems when the underlying database doesn't reflect the needed data elements. Vendors must have built a special consideration for data model extensions as a part of their product.

The Technology and IT Governance Hurdle

One of the biggest misunderstandings about the evolution of companies toward service-oriented architectures is all that's needed is to buy an SOA product. SOA is not a single product, but an architectural approach designed to support maximum flexibility and reuse of existing assets.

Companies that successfully deploy SOA will use technologies they may already have and combine them with new infrastructure to deliver on the SOA vision. As such, several technologies are vital to SOA plans. Combined in a well-coordinated fashion, they form the foundation of an SOA framework that delivers new and distinct composite applications.

This combined framework (see Figure 6) also represents the next major battleground for infrastructure and application vendors looking to retain or overtake account control of companies, large and small. Companies will be basing their decisions heavily on how well their strategic vendors can deliver against the requirements of an SOA framework. Is the product complete? Is it well integrated? How comprehensive is the ecosystem surrounding the framework?

Think of the framework as a high-level guide to help understand and compare the differences between the technology approaches of prospective vendor partners.

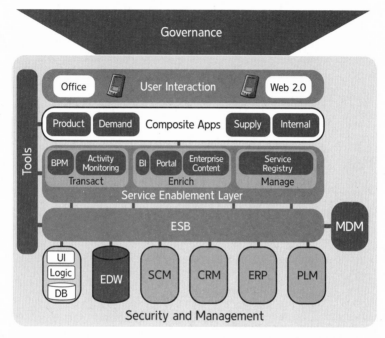

Figure 6: AMR Research SOA framework

The most important element of the framework is also the hardest to pin down from a product standpoint, since governance means different things to different people. Contrary to vendor claims, no one product delivers SOA governance. SOA governance demands companies define and maintain policies on development, deployment, and management of services (where the SOA governance vendors are typically positioned). These services will be tracked in a repository that allows developers to quickly identify services for use in new composites. Linking those policies to the process and technologies used for investment planning and prioritization (like IT portfolio management tools) is also vital. And linking this process to a broader model for the enterprise architecture will help keep shorter term investment cycles consistent with the longer term enterprise architecture vision.

Another key aspect is an organization's ability to measure the value created by the different services based on their utilization versus cost. This will bring together tools from the IT operations group for financial management and configuration management. Together these tools give organizations the ability to do lifecycle planning and optimization of the services deployed to meet business requirements or governance.

The role of tools

Each element of the framework is likely to provide tooling to allow for the modeling, creation, deployment, or management of these services. Consider the following examples:

- Process modeling—Organizations will need to be able to quickly identify new process flows and model them against the set of services.

- Key performance indicator monitoring—Distinct from operations monitoring, these tools help map business performance indicators to process flows to determine whether business is performing according to plan. They set corrective actions to manage unplanned events.

- Service repository—Lets developers identify and reuse common services.

- Administration and security—Set the overall configuration for the SOA framework and how it will be managed and secured.

Service enablement layer

The service enablement layer is a conceptual term to aggregate the technologies that most directly are required to create new and distinct composite applications. This is also the layer that most likely will require the most incremental investment as business process management, business activity monitoring (BAM), and service registry tools are still in the early stages of adoption. The service enablement layer is divided into three categories:

- Transact—The technologies that are essential to delivering the core transactional abilities of a composite application. BPM provides the orchestration and execution of process flows, and BAM delivers the event management and monitoring to ensure that the flows are delivering desired outcomes.

- Enrich—When combined with the core transaction capabilities, the technologies of this segment will ultimately deliver the distinction from previous generations of applications. The ability to integrate business intelligence information into the process flow, support structured and unstructured content in the same composite, and take advantage of portals for presence and collaboration will help create applications that truly operate in the context of how people want to work.

- Manage—All potential benefits are useless if the composite applications are unreliable. A service registry is important to help operationally manage the services, describing their performance characteristics and their relationship in a composite application.

Underpinning the service enablement layer is a distributed integration platform that supports the existing integration needs of applications and requirements of new composites. ESB is a standards-based platform that provides messaging, transformation, monitoring, and content-based routing.

What makes it distinct from previous generations of integration technology is its ability to use standard technologies like XML to abstract the applications from how they send and receive data through the bus. This technology holds the promise to break the cycle of having to update every integration connection point when a new application is installed or an existing application is enhanced.

Often lost in the SOA hype and its focus on services is the notion of maintaining consistency of the data. Master data management (MDM) is an essential component of any SOA framework because it synchronizes data on customers, products, suppliers, materials, and business processes. Given the distributed nature of a composite application, an SOA without MDM would be neither manageable nor scalable. It is highlighted as a distinct element because its utility spans the existing monolithic enterprise applications and new generations of composites.

New Delivery Models and Licensing in the Software Industry | 4

New Delivery Models and Licensing in the Software Industry

Licensing and delivery models within the software industry over the past few years have seen some of their most rapid evolution and subsequent turmoil since the advent of client/server. For years, the choice between named and concurrent user licensing was often the biggest decision. Although vendors began moving to browser-based interfaces in the 1990s, the licensing didn't change much.

Then came software as a service, composite application architectures, and rising support and maintenance costs, which led software buyers to begin challenging the old ways. And while new licensing, subscription, maintenance, and delivery models offer software buyers more options than ever before, they still lack consistency in terminology, measurements of total cost of ownership, and even budgeting methods. This is leaving many buyers confused and frustrated, as seen in the dramatic opinion changes in the past two years about the old ways versus the new ones.

State of the Union for License Software Models

Executives who buy and use enterprise applications are very dissatisfied with the licensing and maintenance policies of their key software vendors, a 2004 AMR Research survey found. The revelation set off alarms at software companies, which began to realize an end to payments for maintenance and upgrades would destroy the fundamental business model of the enterprise application market.

In that survey, we found that less than one-third of respondents were happy with their vendor's policies, and a high percentage of companies were considering dropping maintenance or even switching application vendors. In an environment where most application software companies generate 80 percent or more of their revenue from existing customers, this was frightening news.

Opinions, plans, and policies started changing among buyers and sellers throughout 2004. A year later, a similar survey with more than 300 IT and business executives found a remarkably huge shift in attitude (see Figure 1).

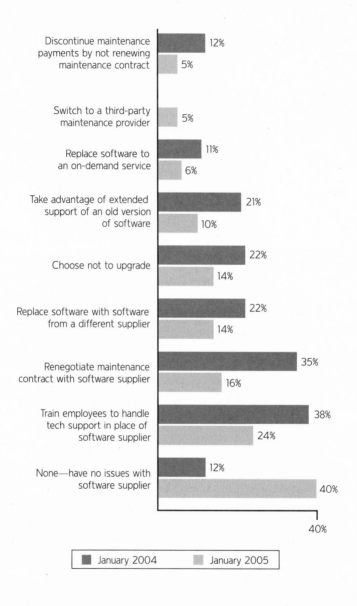

Figure 1: Actions planned to take in the next 12 months
to counter issues with major software suppliers

The number of companies that had no issues with their software suppliers increased more than 300 percent. The one exception to the dramatic change in attitude was third-party maintenance, in which 5 percent of the respondents said they intended to switch software vendors. While the number of companies offering these services is definitely increasing, their impact on the enterprise application market will continue to be very modest.

No buyer consensus on licensing

Companies continue to be unhappy with the complexity and obscurity of their vendors' licensing structures. Complaints are far more prevalent about how the software is licensed than about the actual price of the software. Meanwhile, the entire software industry is struggling to find a sustainable business model that lets software firms charge for the use of intellectual property without annoying customers or driving away prospects. One of the real issues for vendors is that software buyers can't seem to agree on what kind of licensing scheme they prefer.

Larger groups of buyers favor very different types of licensing, and even that varies a great deal based on the application category. The survey found 23 percent of respondents advocated the highly variable "usage-based" or "on-demand" approach, while 26 percent wanted "site licensing," where they pay a flat fee without regard to the number of users or how much of the product is used. Another large segment (20 percent) prefers a middle road that involves a one-time license fee based on the number of users, which is a relatively nonvolatile metric.

What is evident is the correlation between licensing preference and the stability of the business. Those organizations that are highly cyclical or growing rapidly tend to favor licensing that is tied to actual usage, while more stable and predictable companies love site licenses, where there are no surprises. The position and personality of the respondent also has a major influence. CIOs prefer less variable licensing approaches because it makes their planning and budgeting task much easier. They dread the idea of having to go to the CFO in the middle of the year for more money because some business activity has triggered a software usage metric. By contrast,

departmental or divisional user executives love the idea of only paying for what they use and are typically unsympathetic about the IT
department's budgeting problems.

What this means for vendors is that they can't simplify their
licensing structure by standardizing on a single approach. It may
make more sense to offer customers a choice of licensing schemes
based on their preference, company culture, or even the maturity of
the implementation. The real complications will come when existing customers decide that they want to switch from one method to
another. Take the enterprise resource planning (ERP) vendor that
also sells customer relationship management (CRM) systems, for
example. A large number of suite vendors use a variety of license
structures and metrics for parts of their product even when it is sold
to a customer as an integrated suite. This always confuses the buyer
and creates a negative impression about the vendor that probably
can't be justified by whatever incremental revenue it may generate.

Looking for alternatives

In 2004, a large number of companies were considering dropping
payments for support and updates from their software vendors. Since
maintenance revenue often represents 40 percent or more of an
enterprise software vendor's revenue, this could have profoundly
changed the industry. And while the 2005 survey found customers
much happier in general, with 74 percent of the respondents still
buying support from their software vendors, interest in third-party
support is clearly growing (see Figure 2).

When asked about their preference for maintenance and support,
18 percent said they would like to buy it from a third party. Until recently, the software vendors didn't need to be particularly concerned
about this interest because only a handful of very small companies
offered maintenance contracts for enterprise applications. SAP's
acquisition of TomorrowNow raised the profile of the industry in
the United States, but the real threat to application vendors is likely
to come from IT service providers in India and other areas with an
abundance of low-cost technical skills. These firms have tended to
focus on development and system integration work, but they would
undoubtedly be happy to offer annual support contracts as a way to

develop or extend their relationship with large corporations. As composite applications grow, they could become the new powerhouses by developing service-oriented architecture (SOA)-based custom applications that tack on to base ERP and other packaged systems.

Many of the Indian IT service firms are already providing 24-hour support for applications as a part of managed services or outsourcing contracts. Through these activities, plus implementation and upgrade consulting, they have developed a highly trained staff of experts on most of the major software packages. If 18 percent of enterprise application buyers really prefer to buy support, bug fixes, updates, and even enhancements from someone other than their software vendor, this is clearly a major opportunity for India, Inc. and other service firms (see Chapter 5 for more on the changing role of services).

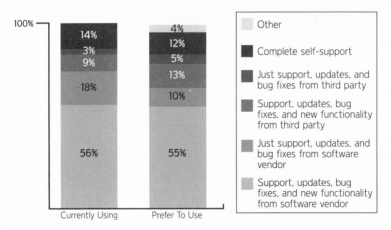

Base: January 2005 respondents currently using applications (n=242)

Figure 2: Software maintenance policies, January 2005

Record maintenance rates are worth the price

The price of application maintenance continues to rise in spite of customer resistance and a slower software market. Companies are reporting that their average maintenance contract is now priced at 19 percent of total software license fees, and even higher in some segments. Despite the price, a high percentage of companies feel they get good value for the maintenance expense (see Figure 3).

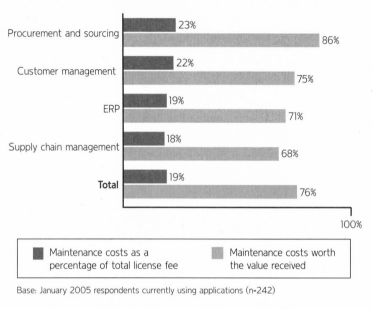

Base: January 2005 respondents currently using applications (n=242)

Figure 3: Maintenance costs as a percentage of total license fee versus maintenance costs worth the value received

In fact, the more companies spend on maintenance (on a percentage basis), the more convinced they are that it is worth the money. This was one of the few areas where there was a significant difference in attitude based on the size of company. When asked whether companies felt that their application software maintenance was delivering good value for the support received, small companies were much more likely to say "yes" than larger organizations. 92 percent of companies with annual revenue of less than $250 million felt they were getting good value, while only 76 percent of midsize companies ($250 million to $1 billion) and 70 percent of enterprises larger than $1 billion felt the same. Larger companies tend to be satisfied with the quality of the support, but unhappy with the price. In most cases, they feel they don't use the vendors' support organization enough to justify the expense, and are more likely to view it as an insurance policy.

Heads up—change is coming

While our survey certainly suggests that application software customers are much happier with their vendors than they were a year ago, it appears that change is coming. There is still considerable dissatisfaction with the very confusing licensing structures that are in place and a rapidly growing interest in on-demand pricing. AMR Research recommends that vendors begin offering usage-based pricing as an option before they find themselves having to react to their competitors. Buyers that have an interest in this form of pricing should request that their vendors propose subscription pricing as well as their conventional licensing approach. The important thing for buyers is to look beyond the attractiveness of no upfront investment. Often these contracts include other terms that may establish minimum spending levels, drive increased volatility, or allow rapid price escalation. Most companies don't have much experience with evaluating or negotiating these types of agreements, and they should be especially cautious.

State of the Union for the SaaS Model

The concept of paying for application software based on actual usage is more than 30 years old, but it was largely replaced by perpetual licenses after computer "time-sharing" died in the 1980s. Recently, large infrastructure vendors have thrown their marketing muscle behind the concept, and salesforce.com has signed up a half-million subscribers for its customer management products.

The software-as-a-service (SaaS) model really started to take hold three years ago, starting in CRM. It was a rather simple concept. Salespeople could subscribe to a contact management or sales force automation (SFA) application for a monthly fee, using it through a browser on their desktop. The IT organization had some initial reservations, but the model was isolated mostly to small businesses or remote divisions of larger organizations.

The past year has seen SaaS starting to take off as vendors across application categories flock to it—each with its own business model, architecture, and terminology. This is new territory for all involved. While the Wild West of SaaS has some great advantages for buyers, the old methods for buying, budgeting, and paying for software no longer apply.

Everybody is talking about it, but few are really doing it

While there has been a great deal of press coverage of the concept, very few major applications outside of CRM are offered this way. Many people confuse hosting with on demand, but in most hosting situations, companies must purchase the software licenses before arranging for the software vendor or a third party to run the applications for them. An AMR Research survey found 9 percent of respondents are paying for some applications on an on-demand or usage basis, but on demand still represents less than 3 percent of revenue for the enterprise application market.

However, when we surveyed users on how they wanted to purchase applications in the future, we saw a very different pattern (see Figure 4). Many of the companies that are currently licensing applications based on user seats believe in the future they will be paying for applications based on actual usage.

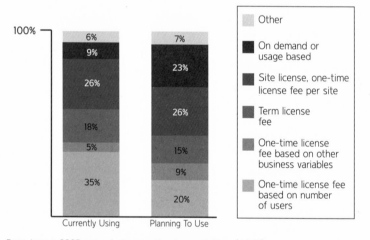

Base: January 2005 respondents currently using applications (n=242)

Figure 4: Software license structure, January 2005

The fact that 23 percent of the executives surveyed indicated that their preferred method for purchasing enterprise applications is on demand should be a wake-up call for software executives who have mostly been taking a wait-and-see or marketing-only approach to on demand.

The preference for on demand varies considerably by type of application, but in each segment the percentage of companies that wants to switch from user-based licensing to on demand has increased significantly. Even in ERP, where perpetual licensing based on user seats has been the accepted standard for more than 20 years, 14 percent of the executives surveyed said they would like to switch to on demand.

Users may be ready for SaaS, but most vendors are not

Application software vendors have been flirting with schemes that would allow customers to pay for their applications based on actual usage, but very few established software vendors are ready to offer a true SaaS option. Even the high-profile success of salesforce.com has not convinced most of the leading vendors to rearchitect their applications. But it's not strictly a technology issue. Part of the problem is that the software industry has grown up with a business model based on collecting large license fees at contract signing, and then charging 15 to 20 percent per year for maintenance and support. If a vendor suddenly switched to usage-based fees, it could see a dramatic drop in revenue. While in the long run these companies might generate the same total revenue per customer with much better predictability, the initial revenue plummet scares them.

The vendors also struggle with the problem of compensating and motivating their sales reps in a SaaS environment. The typical enterprise application salesperson is used to getting huge commissions from a small number of very large license transactions. Gradual monthly payments based on a customer's usage fees just don't excite these elephant hunters very much. The same problem exists for vendors with established indirect sales channels, where partners are used to capturing an upfront margin on software sales. Many are also struggling with their legacy value proposition of technology and implementation skills, which become dramatically devalued in a SaaS sale.

Corporate culture also seems to play a role in a software company's ability to effectively deliver SaaS. While the majority of customer subscriptions for SaaS typically span one or more years, software vendors still need to concern themselves not just with the initial sale, but the ongoing software renewals. While this is seemingly obvious, many traditional software companies have had difficulty making this fundamental shift. This phenomenon has placed a new premium on the value of culture within the software community where customer service, user adoption, and easier implementations are the new gold standards. Metrics formerly relegated to the likes of telecommunications companies—total contract value, customer retention, and churn rates—now pervade the software industry. This is good news for software users, as it forces vendors to put a new premium on customer satisfaction.

However, as more vendors attempt to either make the shift from traditional on-premises software or to a dual delivery model, new architectures, pricing models, and delivery methods are adding to the confusion. At the same time, IT organizations are struggling to determine how SaaS fits into their architecture, and finance departments need to move away from traditional means of budgeting and paying for software. In fact, the majority of deployments are budgeted from line-of-business expense budgets, not from the IT budget. With software as a service, hardware is no longer purchased and depreciated, and total cost of ownership (TCO) calculations have become more difficult to compare on a level playing field.

Effect on the software industry landscape

Customers or prospects expressing an interest in usage-based pricing will probably not be sufficient to get the major application providers to enthusiastically adopt a whole new model. What we are likely to see is smaller vendors or new entrants offering on-demand pricing as a way to distinguish their products and lower the barrier to entry by eliminating the large upfront expense for buyers. In the CRM market, for instance, the rapid growth of salesforce.com, which only offers on-demand pricing, has forced even well-established vendors to create on-demand products. Startup software companies are also finding it much easier to attract venture funding with the recurring revenue business model associated with SaaS.

In the ERP and supply chain markets, none of the leaders seem ready to take the plunge quite yet. Many of the vendors are using value-pricing approaches where they tie license fees to variables other than number of users, but these still require the customer to buy licenses and are not truly SaaS. Some niche products, Linux, and open-source ERP systems are already available as SaaS. A number of vendors with older ERP products in their portfolios are looking to extend the life of those products by offering them on an on-demand basis.

Software as a service has also begun to change software companies' development strategies and schedules. SaaS providers typically perform regular upgrades (some automatic and some scheduled by the customer), and with no custom coding in the equation, the process is relatively seamless and straightforward. In fact, IT representatives often comment that the ease of upgrades is the biggest benefit they see to the SaaS model.

As time goes on, SaaS and SOA will push all software vendors to react much more quickly to customer demand and new business requirements. Software buyers will be less content to wait a year or longer to take a license upgrade or implement a whole new module to address a pressing business issue. And niche functionality can increasingly address smaller groups of users, either as opt-in functions or as per-user incremental charges.

The Software Buyer

More than ever before, software buyers are faced with an increasingly complex decision. Not only do they need to do a thorough feature-and-function analysis, they now have to wade through numerous pricing models and delivery options, and various combinations of both. While they have been bombarded with "marketechture" about software as a service for years now, a lack of standardized terminologies, architectures, and pricing models leave prospective buyers with more questions than answers.

What's in an architecture?

In the nascent stages of SaaS, vendors constantly battled over a multitenancy versus single-tenancy architecture. Multitenancy emerged as the primary distinction between the old (somewhat failed) model of the application service provider (ASP). However, numerous factors led to several new architectures somewhere in between.

The reality is that architectures are mostly important to the pro-viders because they most directly affect their cost of providing the software service. Buyers, on the other hand, should ask questions about pricing models (is there a startup fee?), service-level agree-ments (is there one, and are there explicit rebates?), and customer support (is it included in the monthly fee, and how comprehensive is it?). If the answers to all these questions are favorable, the issue of architecture is reduced to an academic discussion rather than a major decision point.

The Tenets of Tenancy

Multitenancy model

In a pure multitenancy strategy, a single instance of application and data model provides software service to all its customers at once.

The single greatest advantage to a single-tenancy architecture is that it can reach small customers deploying as few as five seats at the same price per user as larger deployments. The model, in the spirit of true SaaS, allows a customer to scale the application usage (and fees) up or down to meet its needs.

Customer support can be much more easily managed, since only a single version of the software is live at any given time. However, any problem with the single instance means a problem for most or all customers, and outages tend to occur during peak usage periods.

Hybrid-tenancy model

At its most basic level, a hybrid architecture takes the best character-istics from single and multitenancy to host individual instances of an application for each unique customer, while taking advantage of some of the cost-reducing methodology from multitenancy.

In many cases, customers basically remain on the same version, mini-mizing support and quality assurance costs. On the other hand, the ability of customers to migrate on their own accord creates more flexibility for customers, but raises support costs and complexity.

The hybrid-tenancy model lets the application provider charge monthly fees without the big startup costs, which plagued the traditional ASP model. While the specifics vary in terms of each vendor's approach, most point to the sense of security assured by individual customer instances, and that the likelihood of outages across the entire customer base would be dramatically reduced.

However, the drawback to this model is the higher cost of adding incremental customers. Some vendors sidestep this problem by only pursuing customers with 100 or more users. Other vendors switch to a multitenancy model for smaller customers.

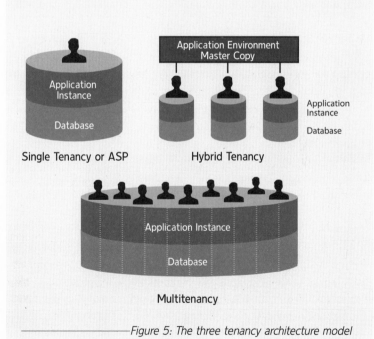

Figure 5: The three tenancy architecture model

While many early SaaS deployments started out as temporary fixes, few companies have dropped their on-demand for on-premises software deployments. Buyers are now more likely to be concerned about the long-range differences in total cost of ownership between the two options. Some of the elements are similar with regard to cost and how they are budgeted, but most are very different. For one, there are differing cost components for each model in the first year and subsequent years of usage (see Table 1). While the dollar amounts of each line item will vary by company and situation, this illustrates some of the cost items to be considered to make a fair comparison of each. Don't necessarily assume that SaaS is more expensive over the long run, and ignore blanket statements about what the breakeven point is. Each situation is unique, so vendor-supplied TCO models should be taken with a grain of salt.

To customize or not to customize

One of the biggest factors in the success of SaaS is also now one if its biggest detractions. In the early days, many found the simplicity of the user interfaces to be a refreshing change from increasingly complex applications. While SaaS may still not offer the same level of customization as resident applications, even highly configured deployments retain the advantage of being seamlessly upgraded at no additional cost.

While customization of SaaS applications are increasing, organizations looking to heavily modify code and retain ownership of the intellectual property should stick to deploying software behind the firewall.

However, many companies believe their business processes are more unique than they really are. They should weigh the advantages to more custom-coded logic against the lower maintenance and upgrade costs of using business process tools and configuration instead of customization. Few companies look back in retrospect and say, "I wish I'd done more custom coding."

Cost Element	Year-One Costs		Subsequent Annual Costs	
	SaaS	On premises	SaaS	On premises
Annual subscription/license	√	√	√	
Application implementation	√	√	√	√
User administration	√	√	√	√
Training	√	√	√	√
Hardware		√		
Data center space		√		√
Middleware/database license		√		
Middleware/database implementation		√		
Application support		√		√
Middleware/database support		√		√
Hardware management resources		√		√
Software management resources		√		√

Table 1: Cost elements of SaaS and on-premises software

SaaS is here to stay

Interest in the SaaS model is growing, with human capital management and customer management vendors seeing the most success because of the narrow focus of their products and the importance of usability in applications in which adoption is always a major issue.

In the next several years, many, if not most, of the enterprise application vendors will begin to offer SaaS as a delivery option along with perpetual, term, and enterprise licenses. Entry has no real barrier, and no vendor will be willing to lose a sale simply because the prospect preferred to have the software hosted and pay for it monthly.

The conventional wisdom is that SaaS will appeal to small and midsize companies, while large enterprises will choose conventional licensing. Not so fast. Many larger organizations like the SaaS model but are uncomfortable with the idea of multitenancy, wanting the option of bringing the software in house or having it hosted by a third party if the vendor gets in trouble or is unhappy with the service level.

If major ERP vendors begin to offer SaaS, some of these larger companies may find it very useful for fast-track deployments, smaller or very autonomous business units, or even as a helpful option when the business has a strong sense of urgency but limited appetite for capital expenditure.

The New Role of
Service Providers
and System Integrators 5

The New Role of Service Providers and System Integrators

Resource pressures and a perpetually shifting service provider landscape are forcing companies to reassess their enterprise application implementation and care-and-feeding strategies. It's a seller's market in some respects—the largest global enterprise resource planning (ERP) implementations, for example—and a buyer's market in others. As a result, we're seeing the emergence of best-of-breed service provider sourcing.

Facing difficulty in accessing and retaining resources, business press buzz and executive management pressures regarding India, Inc., ongoing mergers and acquisitions and private equity activity, endangered implementations, and managed services and outsourcing contracts gone wrong, companies reexamining core competencies are all leaning toward a service partner reexamination and reshuffling that will be sustained in the near term to midterm.

To help understand the market, this chapter includes recommendations and analysis that clarify what the enterprise application skill requirements are and will be, which service providers are equipped to help with different types of engagements, and what to expect in contract negotiations when pursuing a multivendor sourcing strategy for enterprise application integration and support services. We also take a look at India's place in emerging technologies like service-oriented architectures, and what role they will play with future service needs.

ERP Consultants and Service Providers: Take Care Along the Multivendor Sourcing Path

PART
ONE

ERP skills generally will continue to be in high demand. 2005 spending data showed 71 percent of companies planned to increase their ERP spending in 2006, with a weighted average budget increase for ERP applications of 14.6 percent. Companies claim roughly a third of their ERP activities are being associated with new implementation projects. At the operational end of the spectrum, instance consolidation and centralization initiatives continue apace.

Companies realize their third-party service options for supporting these activities are more diverse and numerous than ever before. The question becomes how to take advantage without bursting into flames on the risk and cost front.

Service provider universe expanding—or is it?

Two dynamics cause a company's universe of potential enterprise application service providers to contract or expand: the scale and complexity of the undertaking, and the company's internal sourcing and program management maturity.

Depending on the individual client circumstance at a single enterprise application lifecycle point in time, service provider options can be either wildly diverse or extremely limited. For example, for the largest global implementations of a full SAP footprint, accompanied by major business process overhaul and applications management post go-live, there's currently a sole-sourced club of two: Accenture and IBM. At the other extreme, for small-scale technical staffing requirements, there are hundreds of choices.

Customer requirements that lead to the first scenario are rare. The vast majority of enterprise application users today have multiple requirements falling somewhere in between the two. Companies that invest in sourcing and program management skills are in the best position to pursue a multivendor strategy that addresses these diverse requirements. Those that aren't ready to make a serious commitment to this are better off sticking with a single service provider.

Investing in sourcing and program management also helps companies internally align. An informed negotiation stance ensures that service providers are compelled to do the same on their behalf. When a potential customer understands the ultimate goal of large service providers is to control as much of the agenda as possible—from consulting through implementation and managed services, as well as IT and business process outsourcing—it introduces unique opportunities and points that can be leveraged.

In a single-source strategy, the client's primary considerations are cost, flexibility and leverage, resources, and domain competencies. In a multivendor scenario, negotiation discussions should expand to address the more complex issues of overall agreement structure, governance, clear role definitions, collaboration, and accountability.

Take care

Large enterprise application customers are eager to take advantage of global delivery and the cost-dampening aspect of engaging multiple service providers (for those who aren't eager, their CFOs and procurement departments likely beg to differ). However, many overestimate their internal program management skills or have unreasonably optimistic expectations about what it takes to develop them.

There's also the question of whether the client has the stomach and political wherewithal to manage multiple large service providers simultaneously. Successful coalitions of the willing at the high end of the IT services market are as rare as they are in geopolitics.

Market pressure on enterprise application staffing and services will continue for some time, as indicated by AMR Research's quantitative and qualitative data, as well as its direct client experience through our contract negotiation service. Companies with large packaged application footprints, as well as those headed in that direction, should view their service provider sourcing, negotiation, and program management function as a crucial investment.

India's Role in Global ERP and SOA Services

AMR Research's 2006 visit to the major high-technology cities of India to meet with the big IT services firms didn't turn up major surprises as it has in years past. What we did find is that Indian firms' services continue to expand and deepen, and the traditional Big Six global firms keep improving their use of Indian resources.

The Indian firms' approach to service-oriented architectures (SOAs) illustrates their developing industry domain expertise.

Companies with strong business consulting practices (see Stage 4 in Figure 1), such as IBM and Accenture, have developed SOA practices that evaluate existing business strategy and processes, identifying the ones that require the flexibility of SOAs, redesign the practices, and create the SOAs and technical underpinnings to support the strategy. The firms supplement their business processes expertise with templates and tools to streamline the strategy-to-implementation journey.

The Indian firms at the forefront are moving from Stage 2, process implementation, to Stage 3, process optimization. Most of their work to date has been using SOA technology as an integration platform. However, some are expanding their SOA consulting beyond integration projects, heading toward business process reengineering.

125

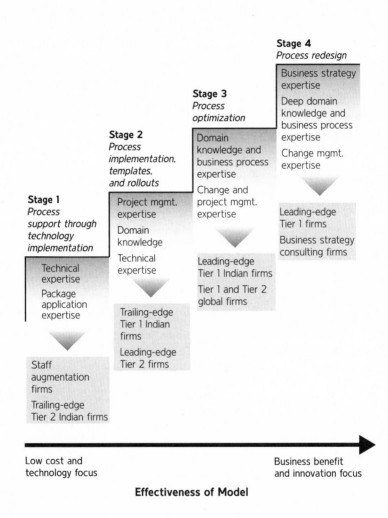

Figure 1: Business process consulting maturity model

Services for services

Patni, an Indian services firm, recently conducted a survey of its customers and found that 27 percent—the top response—identified service-oriented architectures as the area in which they were most likely to substantially invest within the next two years. When the responses for SOA-related activities of web services (16 percent) and business service management (11 percent) are added to the SOA responses, the total rises to more than half.

Consulting and system integration companies are meeting this demand with services built on SOA concepts and emerging SOA standards. Although none of the Indian firms have done any enterprise-wide, SOA-based process transformation projects, they have implemented interesting custom applications built on SOA concepts and technologies. To date, their work has primarily been aimed at filling in the application gaps left by the major enterprise application backbones and dominant best-of-breed products.

Some of the projects discussed by the Indian service providers include the following:

- For a retail company, Infosys created an SOA-based framework that integrated web-based order processing with in-store order processing. It was extended to mobile devices, creating an integrated, multichannel sales model.

- For a European wireless telecom company, Patni created an integration bus, using TIBCO, BEA, and Siebel/Oracle products. The new integration framework allows the company to more rapidly introduce custom products in nine geographies.

- For a large automotive company, Wipro created a BEA Weblogic-based SOA application that integrated data from multiple applications in order to create a system of record for incentive data. This has allowed the company to better manage its incentive spend.

127

In all three cases, the service providers used resources developed within their SOA centers of excellence. In these centers, the companies are investing in tools to implement the emerging SOA standards, training personnel on those tools and standards, and developing proof of concepts that can be used to jump-start projects. Companies interested in moving toward an SOA future can get started on point projects that don't involve massive process reengineering, but do deliver strong returns on investment.

Indian firms getting strategic with enterprise application services

In enterprise application services, Indian firms are moving up the consulting maturity curve and engaging in more strategy work. While strategic business process consulting, on a large scale, is still immature, ERP implementation and rollouts are standard stuff, having come a long way the past few years, expanding their ranks significantly in these practices. More than just adding bodies, the companies are more involved in process optimization projects. Consider the following:

- Cognizant, which only recently developed an SAP practice, built an SAP NetWeaver-certified radio frequency identification (RFID)-based system for yard logistics.

- Tata Consultancy Services (TCS) is implementing business process best practices for a hypermarket retailer using SAP software.

- Satyam detailed its role in a global Oracle application implementation for a worldwide healthcare organization that included developing process requirements, project-managing the implementation, and pushing change management within the organization.

While the Indian companies are not ready to do strategic business consulting, they are demonstrating new abilities that let them support more tactical process optimization projects as well as implement and roll out ERP systems more effectively.

Offshore is dead—long live global delivery maturity and business process expertise

Distinguishing between companies based on India headquarters versus non-India headquarters is no longer relevant. The distinction is now about level of maturity for global service delivery. All of the Tier 1 global services companies—Accenture, BearingPoint, Capgemini, CSC, EDS, HP, and IBM—are investing in global delivery models.

At our last count:

- Accenture has more than 15,000 employees in India, compared to just 200 four years ago. Its Bangalore center is the company's single largest global site.

- Deloitte's Hyderabad facility occupies four prime buildings, and continues to expand. In addition to supporting global delivery services for clients, the operation also houses back-office operations for Deloitte's U.S. business.

- HP, which has more than 20,000 employees in India, has fully integrated its Indian employee base into its global operations.

- IBM has more than 35,000 employees in India, including one of the largest SAP practices in the country.

The leading-edge firms in both groups are stretching toward Stage 4 maturity, but none have mastered the equation on a global scale. Once they do, however, the Indian firms will face formidable competition, forcing them to refine their value proposition well beyond labor arbitrage. Aware of this threat, the Indian firms are looking at automation of processes as the next step. For example, HCL Technologies has developed tools to automate and improve knowledge transfer—usually the weak link in offshore projects.

129

Addressing infrastructure problems

Recent reports have cast a doubt on India's ability to support the hyper-growth of its services business. Horror stories abound of the traffic and infrastructure problems created in the high-tech cities because of growth. But progress is being made, with the problems being addressed:

- An eight-lane road is being constructed in Chennai to serve the high-tech corridor. It will be a race to complete the road because TCS is building a 21,000 person facility at the same time.

- In Hyderabad, a new six-lane road serves its high-tech corridor, greatly reducing traffic problems.

- Bangalore continues to have massive traffic problems, but some small road improvements are having an effect. The commute to Electronics City has not become any worse despite the increase in traffic.

Of greater concern is a recent report that India won't be able to supply enough qualified workers by the end of the decade, but some of this is overblown. Today only an estimated 10 percent of college engineering graduates have the skills necessary to work for the major services firms. However, they have launched internal training programs and joint programs with universities in order to increase this yield to 25 percent, which should eliminate any looming labor shortage.

With the expanding reach of the Indian firms and the maturing global delivery of the Big Six, it's becoming harder to distinguish between the firms based on where their headquarters are located. The designation of "offshore firm" is becoming increasingly meaningless. All firms today have varying levels of non-U.S.-based resources and abilities. India is no longer considered exotic, but rather the source of leading talent.

The Future:
Enterprise Applications
in 2010 and Beyond   6

The Future: Enterprise Applications in 2010 and Beyond

There is much that threatens to alter the enterprise application market as we know it: the consolidation of enterprise application vendors, the entrance of private equity dollars, the move to service-oriented architectures (SOAs), and the growing ability of service firms to fill technology holes in business needs. Let's also not forget the encroachment of consumer technology, like wikis and blogs, and new delivery models, like software as a service (SaaS).

So what will the enterprise application market look like in 2010 as these forces and the ones to come play out? Will it look a lot like today, or are we headed for a brave new world of custom-built applications layered onto packaged transactions systems? Will enterprise resource planning (ERP) be the backbone or the underbelly? Will SAP or Oracle wield all the power, or is the power base moving to India, Inc.?

The answer depends on who you ask. This debate will shape the market the next five years. To frame the argument, we present two very different views from AMR Research's most senior analysts on where things are headed. In Part 1, Jim Shepherd argues it will be business as usual in the enterprise application market. In Part 2, Bruce Richardson says we may be witnessing the death of packaged applications. Check back in 2010 to see who won.

Safety First

by Jim Shepherd

Enterprise applications have steadily expanded their scope and functionality since their emergence in the early 1980s. In many industries, they support and control nearly every business process—and virtually no transaction can be done without software. In a 2006 survey of midsize and large companies in North America and Europe, AMR Research found that 46 percent of employees were licensed to use the ERP system, and most respondents had aggressive plans to extend their deployment. Most organizations will have implemented enterprise applications for every process by 2010, and very few jobs won't require the use of the business system.

This growing ubiquity is certainly the strength of the enterprise application market, but it will also constrain the introduction of new concepts and technologies. Most business executives are simply not interested in experimenting with a system that runs their operations, controls their data, and helps keep them legally compliant. Cool new technologies may be fine for social networking or surfing the web, but the idea of using these technologies for financial management or processing customer orders will be met with very strong resistance. Enterprise applications are now part of the establishment.

Most CIOs these days are not technology enthusiasts. They aren't even likely to have a background in IT, most instead having been promoted from a business position such as finance or operations management. Their job is to manage IT costs, deliver excellent service, and minimize risk to the business. These are not the kind of people who are inclined to rip and replace multimillion dollar systems or experiment with the introduction of new computing concepts. They are also highly unlikely to favor small, innovative startup firms over giant, well-established enterprise application companies.

2010 will look a lot like today

The enterprise application business has been successful because most buyers like the idea of purchasing standard packaged software that supports legal requirements and prevailing business processes. They love the fact they can keep these systems in place for 15 to 20 years, with software vendor support and periodic functional and technological updates. Introducing change into organizations is difficult, expensive, and risky, and most executives like the fact that enterprise applications are stable and quite difficult to change. In most cases, they would like to get fewer updates less often.

In the past five years, we have seen very strong movement toward standardization and centralization of enterprise applications. Companies are establishing shared service centers for human resources, finance, procurement, and customer service. They are also deploying comprehensive enterprise applications to support these functions globally. Most CIOs are actively working to reduce the diversity in their application portfolios, forcing the business to standardize on a very small set of application vendors. Although some may complain that these policies limit innovation, they do promote stability and reliability, as well as reduce the cost of IT and business operations.

What about new technologies?

As enterprise applications get larger and more complex, it becomes nearly impossible for vendors to rewrite their products every time a new technology comes along. The time and cost would be prohibitive, and it is very difficult to convince customers to replace their business systems simply because the vendor has a new version. The major application and infrastructure vendors have spent the past five years trying to generate excitement about SOA with very little success. Application vendors have finally concluded that what most buyers want is a gradual introduction of new technologies and concepts over a series of product updates.

Technology gurus and vendors alike tried to sell SOA by suggesting that, in the future, companies would have infinite flexibility. They would, the story went, have the ability to orchestrate a library of software components into new innovative business processes and build their own applications without conventional programming. Many potential buyers were horrified at the concept. They don't want to buy a box of components and a modeling environment any more than most car buyers want a pile of parts and a toolkit. The vast majority of enterprise application buyers want a complete, fully assembled product. They certainly want to be able to configure and reconfigure it as their business changes. In most cases, however, they would be happy if they never have to build and maintain a single piece of custom software.

The major application vendors are continuing to rebuild their products with SOAs, but they have changed their message and approach to introducing it. It is being positioned as a nondisruptive technology that will give users more deployment flexibility and make it easier to integrate to third-party applications and external partners. While there is still some discussion about distinct business processes and customized composite applications, it's much quieter.

Not quite a brand new world

The enterprise application market, now 30 years old, has finally · left its wild adolescence behind. The market is dominated by large, publicly traded companies that tend to be risk averse, and this suits the majority of the buyers that count on these applications to manage their most sensitive information and processes. Five years from now, the enterprise application market will look much as it does today, except that even more niche vendors will have been absorbed. The dominant products will be broad integrated suites that cover virtually all business functions in an organization. Undoubtedly, the technology will be more modern and products easier to use and deploy, but it won't be a brand new world.

Jim Shepherd brings more than 30 years of manufacturing, operations, and software industry experience to his role as senior vice president at AMR Research. He has helped develop AMR Research's coverage of ERP and led the company's effort to establish the Supply Chain Council and define the SCOR Model.

The Death of Packaged Software

by Bruce Richardson

In any market, being a historian is usually easier and safer than being a prognosticator. This is especially true in the world of enterprise applications. That said, here are my predictions: by 2010, the market will have shifted away from the ERP-centric model that has dominated IT spending the past 15 years. New flexible technologies will move businesses closer to a do-it-yourself IT architecture. For the market leaders of the next decade, it won't be business as usual. The revolution underway is as radical as the shift from gasoline-powered cars to hydrogen, so fasten your seatbelts.

To prove it, let's look at the future from three perspectives: increased pressure to reduce the total cost of ownership but still accelerate innovation, the emergence of next-generation infrastructure, and the rapid shift to a new paradigm of model-based software development.

Total cost of ownership

An IBM executive once said for every dollar spent on applications software, you'll spend $10 integrating the package into other software. Over the lifetime of the application, you'll spend 100 times the original cost to maintain and support the initial investment. Can you prove it?

Consider this: an executive at a well-known Fortune 100 company said he was looking to upgrade to the newest release of his company's ERP system. His team estimated that the new software would provide $10 million in value for $1 million in new licenses. While the benefits outweighed the license fees 10 to 1, enthusiasm was dampened by the services costs. The initial estimate was that the upgrade would cost $90 million over two years. When we repeated this anecdote to another Fortune 100 client, he said that his company had a similar experience, but his ERP upgrade was going to cost an estimated $100 million in services over two years.

To be fair, the widespread adoption of ERP allowed buyers to streamline their architectures. The downside has been a radical increase in complexity that restricts innovation.

Web 2.0 and next-generation infrastructure

Is it any wonder that large companies with huge ERP investments are eager to learn more about how service-oriented architectures might reduce maintenance and upgrade costs? Dr. Paul Horn, senior vice president and director of research for IBM Research, uses a hub-and-spoke slide to demonstrate the future of technology. The hub is "web as platform." The spokes include tools (RSS, AJAX, PHP, Ruby), standards (REST, XHTML), technologies (mashups, wikis, tagging, blogs, rich user experience), small pieces loosely joined or remixed, harnessing collective intelligence, architectural participation, services (no packaged applications), software that gets better as more people use it, and lightweight programming models. Does your current ERP vendor see the web as platform? Is it supporting or planning to embrace the same spokes?

Dr. Horn's perspective represents another layer of refinement or granularity to the Web 2.0 discussions that have quickly spread from Silicon Valley to the rest of the world. The cries of "why can't my ERP applications be as easy to use as Amazon.com or my.Yahoo?" are finally being heard.

The new infrastructure will also do a better job integrating the Microsoft Office desktop with business applications, but it's more than tying Microsoft applications to ERP. Instead, users will be demanding tools that facilitate collaboration. These will include broader adoption of portals as the user interface, dashboards, wikis, instant messaging (IM), integrated web-based telephony (VoIP), mashups, social bookmarks, and the like. Right now, most of these tools are standalone. By 2010, these tools and others will be tightly integrated into the total user experience.

This argues the case against continued ERP centricity. Users don't want to learn another set of applications, but they do want access to the data. For 15 years, we have talked about whether ERP vendors can penetrate deeper inside customer companies (that is, sell more seats inside the account). Over that period, it has barely moved from the 10 percent to 20 percent penetration that MRP II, ERP's predecessor, had. And that's not going to change.

Model-based applications based on SOA

For nearly two years, SAP's Peter Zencke has been working on a strategy that will allow his developers to write new applications without using a procedural programming language. Oracle's John Wookey is now talking openly about model-based development as the basis for the new Fusion applications.

Workday, the new venture cofounded by Dave Duffield, the founder and former CEO of PeopleSoft, has already done it. His company boasts that its software was not written in any traditional programming language and is based exclusively on metadata. While little is known about the scalability of the new development tools, Workday executives estimate they have seen an eightfold increase in developer productivity in terms of the ability to generate new functionality as well as in the quality of the software.

The key here is the adoption of a new object model, native web services, and a new service-oriented architecture. The focus shifts from the familiar pillars of enterprise applications (financials, customer relationship management, supply chain management, product lifecycle management, human capital management, and procurement and souring) to end-to-end business processes. The new business processes will likely be mapped against today's ERP functionality, but the new processes will be about more than just transactions—they will have rich analytics and support structured and unstructured data. This is 180 degrees from the classic ERP transactional model.

Recycle over buy new

By 2010, buyers will be a lot savvier about SOAs and native web services, Web 2.0 (and the successor technologies), and model-based design tools. Their conversations will be about creating or extending new business processes, not packaged applications. They will only require a sliver of today's functionality because of the ability to reuse components using service-oriented architectures or create new composite applications.

This will cause a change in the vendor landscape. While IBM has pledged not to compete with its partners in the applications space, it doesn't have to worry if the application market disappears—IBM is quietly acquiring companies with business process expertise. Expect to see other global services and infrastructure competitors follow the same strategy.

This scenario may represent too much change in too short a time period. That's probably true. It could be that the excitement peaks in 2010, followed by several years of dramatic sales activity. That's the way it happened in the ERP market in the 1990s: it launched in 1991, hysteria followed in 1994–1995, but it had a very strong market for the balance of the decade.

Bruce Richardson, AMR Research's chief research officer, brings more than 20 years of experience to AMR Research, most of it analyzing the software industry with a distinct emphasis on ERP and supply chain. Since joining AMR Research in 1988, he has been responsible for spearheading new market research. He has also contributed to the company's analysis of leading market trends in areas such as service-oriented architectures and software as a service.

Appendix: Enterprise Application Markets

Appendix: Enterprise Application Markets

The following is designed to gauge how the topics discussed in this book are affecting the various enterprise application markets. For each market, you'll find a definition of the category, market sizing and growth rates (when available), key players, how the functionality is shifting, what role new business models are playing, the impact new technologies will have on the market, and a look at the future of each.

A few markets are still too new to have detailed numbers on specific vendor sales, or the vendors covering them come from other markets and don't break out the specific numbers for that market in their financial reports. For these markets (business intelligence and performance management, service lifecycle management, B2B e-business, and manufacturing operations), we provide alternative information, such as customer spending data, a list of major players, or general information on the market's growth and size.

Current data also was not available on retail applications, so numbers from 2004–2005 were used. Although there has been some vendor consolidation since then (Retek now a part of Oracle, for example), the growth percentages should give an indication of how individual vendors are doing now. For the rest of the application areas covered, the data uses AMR Research's 2006 Market Analytix data, which surveys market vendors and uses public data to estimate market sizes.

Enterprise Resource Planning

PART
ONE

Enterprise resource planning (ERP) software is the oldest and largest segment of the enterprise application market. ERP systems comprise a tightly integrated suite of business applications organized around a single, central database. Typical ERP functionality supports transaction processing, planning, and data management across a broad range of functional areas, such as human resources, finance, order management, inventory control, procurement, supply chain, and operations management. The basic premise of ERP is that it is faster and more effective to deploy a single-vendor integrated system than to assemble the equivalent from a collection of independent applications and integration technology.

In the mid-1990s, several hundred ERP products were on the market, each targeting particular geographies, industries, and company sizes. Since that time, the market has significantly consolidated, resulting in large global vendors with comprehensive product functionality and specific systems for various industries. These multibillion-dollar software firms now play a dominant role in the entire IT industry through their account control and the high percentage of IT spending on software, hardware, and services that is driven or influenced by ERP projects.

Market size and growth rates

The ERP vendors generated more than $25 billion in total revenue in 2005 and are expected to grow 14 percent in 2006. Some of this growth is the result of increased penetration into new vertical and geographic markets, but it is also due to large ERP vendors buying up niche application companies to fill holes in their products or satisfy industry requirements.

Key players

SAP and Oracle now generate two-thirds of all revenue in the ERP market, and their share is even more dominant among very large global enterprises. While both vendors are also doing well among small and midsize businesses (SMBs), they face much more effective competition from Sage Group, Microsoft, Infor, and Lawson. Of these players, SAP, the market leader, is the only one that has primarily relied on internal development and organic growth. The rest of the companies have grown through multiple acquisitions of smaller ERP vendors and other best-of-breed products.

Shifts in functionality

When ERP systems emerged in the early 1990s, they typically encompassed financials, order management, and manufacturing only, with very little support for the different requirements of particular industries or locations. In the past few years, most vendors have been rapidly expanding their functionality to cover as many areas of the business as possible. This is partly driven by customer demands for a comprehensive single-vendor system, but it also reflects the way ERP software is sold. Most vendors charge for their software by the number of users, and therefore functionality for more departments means more users and more revenue. Large ERP vendors, tired of losing revenue to smaller software companies in areas like procurement and sourcing, supply chain management (SCM), and customer management, began to expand into those areas through internal development and acquisition. The major ERP vendors are now the market leaders in nearly every application category.

Company Name	Revenue, 2004 ($M)	Revenue, 2005 ($M)	Revenue Forecast, 2006 ($M)	Revenue Share, 2004	Revenue Share, 2005	Revenue Share Forecast, 2006	Growth Rate, 2004-2005	Growth Rate Forecast, 2005-2006
SAP	9372	10542	12334	40%	42%	43%	12%	17%
Oracle	2465	5166	6664	10%	20%	23%	110%	29%
Sage Group	1243	1438	1582	5%	6%	5%	16%	10%
Microsoft	775	891	1051	3%	4%	4%	15%	18%
SSA Global	683	733	755	3%	3%	3%	7%	3%
Infor	242	480	576	1%	2%	2%	98%	20%
Geac	445	445	451	2%	2%	2%	0%	1%
Intentia*	403	388	0	2%	2%	0%	-4%	-100%
Lawson *	357	346	740	2%	1%	3%	-3%	114%
Epicor	226	291	385	1%	1%	1%	29%	32%
Subtotal	16212	20721	24538	69%	82%	85%	28%	18%
Total ERP Market	23649	25358	28998	100%	100%	100%	7%	14%

*Lawson acquired Intentia on April 24, 2006.

———— Top ten ERP vendors ranked by 2005 total revenue (incl. est. '06 growth)

151

More recently, ERP vendors began investing heavily in products for specific industries. Customers in traditional ERP markets like manufacturing have become more demanding, and emerging markets like retail, public sector, and financial services expect products that support their practices and business models. This desire to participate in new industries is also behind many of the acquisitions and partnerships in the application market.

Current and emerging business models

ERP's current business model has been around for more than 20 years. Most of the vendors sell their own products through a combination of direct sales representatives and resellers. Customers purchase perpetual software usage licenses based primarily on the number of users and functional scope of the product. Maintenance fees, which cover support and product enhancements, typically cost 17 to 22 percent of the net license fees. In most cases, the necessary IT infrastructure (databases, operating systems, middleware, hardware, and networking) is sold by technology partners, and the consulting and implementation services are provided by some combination of software vendor, consulting partner, and reseller personnel. We estimate the pull-through revenue that ERP sales generate for third parties is three or four times the revenue that is recognized by the ERP vendors themselves. Total spending on ERP-related products and activities probably exceeds $100 billion per year.

We do expect to see some significant changes to the ERP business model over the next several years:

- As the vendors focus more on SMBs, the ERP market will become volume driven and development of reseller channels will become much more important.

- Software as a service (SaaS) will become a common ERP purchasing option, and ERP hosting and managed services will become much more prevalent. This will force ERP vendors to become less product focused and more services focused, likely creating even more competition between the software companies and their services partners.

- Service-oriented architectures (SOAs) will force the ERP vendors to sell application platforms and components based on industry standards. This should create new opportunities for the ERP players, but it also threatens their account control and encourages IT services vendors and others to build competitive applications.

Impact of new technology

Most ERP vendors are in the process of transitioning to SOAs. This should make it easier for customers to configure, deploy, and manage their systems, and it should help them respond more quickly to market and process changes. SOAs will also make it easier for ERP vendors to create tailored products for specific markets, or even individual customers. This will help the vendors penetrate new markets, and it will also encourage them to partner with specialty software vendors. SOAs and technologies like BPEL should make it feasible to quickly create an integrated system using service-based components from multiple vendors. This could dramatically change the structure and economics of the application industry.

Likely future

ERP systems have become a basic business requirement in many industries, and the use of these systems is rapidly moving down-market and into new geographies. Services industries, such as retail, public sector, and financial services, are also beginning to accept the idea of using ERP suites to manage their key business processes. With the ERP market likely to continue consolidating and new businesses emerging, there is no major threat on the horizon. At the moment, most companies are working hard to extend the deployment of ERP to more areas of their business and expand the use of ERP to more employees. We expect the ERP market to continue to grow much faster than the economy.

Human Capital Management

PART
TWO

The human capital management (HCM) application sector supports operational and strategic personnel-related business activities and processes to best align human resources to achieve a company's goals. It includes the following components:

- Core HR—Employee data administration, including self-service and information portals, payroll and benefits participation administration, and automating employee-initiated travel and expense reconciliation.

- Talent acquisition and recruiting—Full-time recruiting and hiring automation as well as contingent workforce and vendor management.

- Employee performance management—The digitization of performance reviews and appraisals, automated skill and capability assessments, incentive management, and succession and career planning.

- Workforce development—Learning management and educational content development and delivery (particularly e-learning), and content's overlap with knowledge management.

- Workforce management—Time and attendance tracking, absence management, workforce scheduling and optimization, and professional services automation.

All of these areas contribute to the ability of a company to do workforce analytics, which is also a growing area of discipline and IT investment.

Market size and growth rates

Tying with customer management for top growth in 2005, HCM is going to be the fastest growing enterprise application segment through 2010, at a compound annual growth rate (CAGR) of just over 10 percent. The attention to HCM and investments in HCM enterprise applications is due to company interest in innovation for competitive advantage, globalization of markets, and productivity advancements, all of which are tied to optimal deployment of human resources. Of note, companies are paying particular attention to performance management and workforce scheduling and optimization, hoping to squeeze the best returns out of their personnel investments in the coming years.

Key players

The three largest players in the HCM enterprise application market—Oracle, SAP, and Kronos—represent almost 60 percent of market sales.

Oracle has become a huge force in the market with its acquisition of HCM leader PeopleSoft and later addition of customer management vendor Siebel, which had a number of HCM modules, as well. With plans to merge all of these products onto the Fusion platform in 2008, Oracle is committed to HCM market leadership. It recently launched a new Applications Unlimited program, which pledges continued enhancement of JD Edwards, Oracle, PeopleSoft, and Siebel applications already on the market, including HCM functionality.

SAP has made considerable strides in recent years in its interfaces and overall usability of its HCM suite. It is also making investments in more strategic HCM areas of acquisition and performance management that tie nicely into its back-end financial systems. The availability of employee self-service in mySAP 2004 and manager self-service in mySAP 2005 provides a pull for many organizations to upgrade their ERP suites, especially as maintenance runs out.

Company Name	Revenue, 2004 ($M)	Revenue, 2005 ($M)	Revenue Forecast, 2006 ($M)	Revenue Share, 2004	Revenue Share, 2005	Revenue Share Forecast, 2006	Growth Rate, 2004-2005	Growth Rate Forecast, 2005-2006
Oracle	324	1395	1534	7%	26%	25%	331%	10%
SAP	1122	1268	1433	23%	23%	24%	13%	13%
Kronos	469	528	586	10%	10%	10%	13%	11%
Sage Group	140	160	160	3%	3%	3%	14%	0%
Lawson	103	104	114	2%	2%	2%	1%	10%
Ultimate Software	72	89	108	1%	2%	2%	23%	21%
Microsoft	70	80	95	1%	1%	2%	15%	18%
Workbrain	51	80	95	1%	1%	2%	56%	18%
Kaba Benzing	76	78	82	2%	1%	1%	3%	5%
Taleo	59	78	94	1%	1%	2%	33%	21%
Subtotal	2486	3859	4300	51%	71%	71%	55%	11%
Total HCM Market	4869	5458	6025	100%	100%	100%	12%	10%

Top ten HCM vendors ranked by 2005 HCM revenue (incl. est. '06 growth)

With more than half a billion in revenue and a long record of growth and profitability, Kronos is well positioned to provide best-of-breed applications. Kronos' strength has been workforce management, but it is expanding into acquisition, performance, and development to round out an entire strategic HCM suite. It recently acquired hourly-recruiting platform developer Unicru toward that goal.

Shifts in functionality

The sub-areas of HCM have seen tremendous consolidation over the past few years as best-of-breed vendors sought to carve out strategic HCM suites ahead of the ERP vendors, which have predominantly been used for core HR implementations.

Since 2005, recruitment has been aligned with other areas of HCM, particularly performance management, in an effort to facilitate improved succession planning among other needs. This led HR portal developer Authoria to acquire Hire.com in June 2005, and initial assessment specialist Kenexa to buy Webhire in January 2006. Meanwhile, leading performance management vendor SuccessFactors is developing its own applicant tracking module. This reflects the ability of performance tools to better identify which employees and in which areas companies should invest, such as competency identification and succession mapping, and then linking it to recruiting.

In the learning management space, consolidation is prevalent among content development and management, learning management, and content delivery vendors. Of note, the largest learning management vendor, SumTotal, which was formed with the merger of Docent and Click2learn in 2004, acquired Pathlore in October 2005. Second largest learning company Saba acquired online collaboration platform vendor Centra in February 2006.

For its part, workforce management is looking to extend HCM's effectiveness in particular segments, with generalists acquiring specialists and specialists acquiring their way into new markets. Kronos acquired SmartTime, a small manufacturing-centric workforce player, in August 2006. Manufacturing and distribution system expert RedPrairie acquired the retail workforce and operations management player BlueCube in July 2006 to extend its vision of the consumer-driven supply in retail. Aftermarket services support system vendor Servigistics acquired TransDecisions for workforce routing and scheduling for the field service and logistics markets in May 2006. Finally, contact center systems specialist NICE Systems added fellow contact center workforce management vendor IEX and contact center performance management specialist Performix in April 2006.

Current and emerging business models

High-value professional services that go beyond integration and implementation are the most significant developments among HCM vendors, particularly for back-office needs. These areas, which are too often neglected for lack of time, resources, or internal expertise, increasingly require more transformational support than software alone can deliver. The professional services from software vendors range from complementary products and complex content tradition-ally offered by separate third parties to business process and best practice consultative services, such as the following:

- As enterprise business applications make the transition to software as a service, companies are more comfortable asking vendors for help in ongoing deployment issues beyond the initial install and integrations.

- The increased comfort with outsourced HR business processes beyond payroll and benefits administration also has paved the way for services. In some cases, this has pressed its demand from companies now offering software in these areas.

- The trend toward incremental outsourcing in lieu of megadeals means that companies want smaller pieces of functionality, as well. This opens the door to smaller work that software providers can take on themselves, and gives companies one source to hold responsible.

- Clients also appreciate the software vendor's narrower focus on the product and domain in question. Third-party consul-tants often get a bad rap for pitching marginal services the client doesn't really want or need.

- Domain expertise is also a big factor. Being on the front lines of any process, from hiring contingent workers to assessing people's performance, provides insight into what defines success. Vendors can also provide a concentrated and committed perspective that internal personnel with lots of competing demands on their time cannot.

Impact of new technology

Companies will cite domain expertise as the main factor in engaging specialist suite vendors, particularly for complex, yet non-core, areas of the back office that face fluctuations in regulations and market dynamics. Making the case that many of these functions need to remain in-house because they are vital is difficult. In many cases, the internal personnel's lack of expertise or time to address these processes will force a shift to third-party support.

As such, HCM applications over the next five years will continue to lead the development and acceptance as SaaS. However, the large installed base of traditionally delivered applications by the ERP vendors, which are increasingly adding more strategic HCM functions, will dampen any wholesale changes in how the technology is delivered.

Service-oriented architectures will also play an increasingly important role, particularly with HCM requiring interactions outside the company. Indeed, nearly every area of HCM involves exchanges with third-party specialists and service providers. For talent acquisition, firms need to share data and workflows with recruitment specialists and candidate agencies. In workforce scheduling, systems need inputs from business demand, like sales. In development, leading learning content comes from educational institutions. In assessment, more companies are using tried-and-true performance metrics from industrial psychologists. SAP users are already seeing early progress in SOA services for benefits administration.

Likely future

With the proliferation of true SOA standards, HCM stands to benefit from best practice processes, policies, and content that can be easily used by organizations to bring HCM in line with strategic business goals. The ability to easily swap out new products through SOA also provides more flexibility to organizations looking to continuously improve HCM asset deployment, which must be an ongoing discipline, not a one-time automation project.

The promise of strategic HCM alignment with business goals can only be achieved as transactional human resource functions are streamlined through shared services, software, and, in many cases, outsourced systems because these free up HCM professionals to think about and act on the strategic HCM questions. Yet as systems supporting the administrative aspect of HR consolidate, the more information these individuals will have at their fingertips to navigate the complex challenges of capitalizing on personnel for business success.

Imagine a rich electronic dossier for each individual contributing to an organization's success, not only populated with the core vital statistics of being an employee—name, address, compensation, benefits, and dependents—but also that individual's career goals and path carefully mapped out and interrelated with the needs of your business. When all of these dimensions are accessible to the business and the employee, the strategic impact of HCM becomes clear.

Business Intelligence and Performance Management

Business intelligence (BI) and performance management (PM) products provide options to query, report, and analyze historical and current activity, but also to project what performance will most likely be, based on causal inputs. The BI/PM market consists of the following distinct buying segments:

- Business intelligence tools—Tools that provide information gathering and analysis to end users.

- Dashboard and scorecards—Tools and/or applications that help businesses track key performance indicators (KPIs) by providing a unified view of organizational performance data and options on a timed or near real-time and integrated basis.

- Planning, budgeting, and forecasting products—Applications that provide a business with a high degree of flexibility to align financial and/or operational plans to its specific enterprise or departmental planning processes.

- Analytic applications—Delivered applications that accurately gather, unify, coordinate, and analyze company-wide or content-specific data.

- Analytic infrastructure—Infrastructure to store, organize, and prepare the system of record for enterprise reporting and analysis. This includes data warehouses/datamarts, data integration (including data cleansing), and multidimensional databases that the company custom built or purchased as a packaged application.

Companies can chose to purchase and/or deploy components of a BI/PM architecture independently or look to software providers for a bundle of products to support as many different abilities as necessary.

Market size and growth rates

Companies will spend nearly $23 billion on performance management projects in 2006. Spending on these projects grew by 3 percent overall from 2005. Some areas are on fire, such as dashboards/scorecards and BI, while others are flat to declining. Customer inquiries point to resurgence in analytic infrastructure issues. Commensurately, we expect this BI/PM category will grow significantly in 2007.

Key players

Market participants are segmented in three major groups:

- Best-of-breed providers—Companies such as Actuate, Business Objects, Cognos, Hyperion Solutions, Information Builders, MicroStrategy, and SAS Institute have at least a decade of experience (and in a couple of cases, nearly 30 years) in the reporting, analysis, and BI/PM realms.

- Enterprise application vendors—Oracle and SAP are reaching beyond their traditional business application roots and augmenting their product lines with BI/PM functionality. In particular, Oracle is using its acquisition strategy—PeopleSoft and Siebel, in particular—to build out its products. Both firms want to own the management of business processes through analysis of business activity.

164

Application Area	2005		2006		2005 to 2006 Growth
	Dollar Spend ($M)	Percentage Spend	Dollar Spend ($M)	Percentage Spend	
Business Intelligence	5775	26%	6352	28%	10%
Analytics Infrastructure	4452	20%	4273	19%	-4%
Dashboards and Scorecards	4145	19%	5223	23%	26%
Planning, Budgeting, and Forecasting	4139	19%	4014	17%	-3%
Analytics Applications	3719	17%	3084	13%	-17%
Total Performance Management	22230	100%	22946	100%	3%

Performance management spending by category, 2005-2006

- Technology platform providers—IBM, Microsoft, and Oracle are using their influence and strength in IT infrastructure to extend into BI/PM product areas.

Buyers today have more options for business intelligence and performance management. Companies have no overwhelming preference for one category or another, but the fact that companies are split indicates a real change in attitude over the past few years. In any case, most companies report they use multiple product categories to support their BI/PM needs.

Shifts in functionality

The biggest barrier to adoption has been making business intelligence and performance management relevant to more users across the business. How do you break through the adoption logjam? Making business intelligence and performance management approachable and easily understandable—for example, walk up and use—is essential. Decision makers overwhelmingly believe that simplicity is the key to eventual ubiquity. Four strategies illustrate the way that business intelligence and performance management is stretching to meet the diverse needs of its many different constituencies:

- Information to the masses—Whether it's simple report viewing, e-mail distribution, or delivery through a corporate portal, getting the right stuff to the right people when they need it fosters broader adoption. Self-service reporting—letting users create reports and inquiries when they need to—is viewed as an important strategy to reduce IT backlog.

- Information in context—Rather than giving users a blank canvas and asking them to paint their own picture, why not deliver vital metrics, analyses, and/or reports in the context of the business activity they perform? Although our spending estimates indicate that analytic applications are less popular this year than last, we expect resurgence of interest in 2007 as richer options become available for all types of business data.

- Information as "sound bites"—Taken together, dashboards and scorecards are hot, so it's no wonder this area has seen phenomenal growth of late. The idea of shrinking pages of data into consumable nuggets is appealing because users can quickly assess the health (or weakness) of a business and/or process area without having to wade through extraneous details. Obviously, drilling into the details when necessary is part and parcel of this approach, but delivering the facts cuts through the clutter and informs users of where they stand.

- Searching for the right information—Rather than teaching the masses to use a new product, why not plug the product into something they already use? The idea of using search to trigger business intelligence and performance management has recently been introduced to the market. Customers find this option attractive as it adapts easily to how they think. This concept also applies to desktop productivity tools, such as spreadsheets, presentations, or word processing documents. Adapting access and delivery to already accepted models will further adoption quickly.

Current and emerging business models

All vendors that participate in this market sell product direct to customers. Best-of-breed vendors have well-established channel sales programs where third parties—other software vendors, consulting partners, or distributors—sell, service, and deliver software assets. In some cases, up to a third of their software license revenue is earned this way.

Increasingly, service providers play an important role in product delivery. More than $7.2 billion is spent on integration and consulting services. Besides traditional implementation services, consultants assist in delivering predefined systems to solve specific analytic needs. For example, HCM outsourcers are also delivering workforce analytic applications as part of the service offered to customers and prospects.

As part of our annual spending survey, we discovered the following shifts in attitude will affect business models in the future:

- Anywhere from 17 to 23 percent of companies, depending on the BI/PM investment area, would prefer a SaaS or on-demand purchase option.

- Service-based companies preferred this model significantly more than manufacturers.

- Difference in demand is insignificant for BI/PM SaaS based on company size.

Some providers presently are dabbling in this area, while other companies are starting up with this as the only model. We expect this to significantly affect the BI/PM market the next few years.

Impact of new technology

Historically, transaction systems captured data and BI systems reported and analyzed that information. This hard separation still exists in some cases, but it is rapidly changing as business users demand analysis everywhere:

- Analyze in context—Deliver information in context of business activity being performed.

- Analysis drives process—When facts are uncovered, automate the process(es) that should follow next.

- Drive analysis from other activities—Business intelligence and performance management are invoked from whatever activity is being performed.

This demand for plug-and-play components is creating significant technical innovation in the BI/PM market. While vendors are at various stages of adoption, this screams out for a service-oriented architecture. Because there are many deployment models in play, vendors need to be able to easily adapt to shifting demands, and SOA is the best alternative for this.

While data integration is a foundational requirement for business intelligence and performance management, increasingly more effort is being placed on standardization and cleansing of data for creation of that definitive source of truth for all types of data—financial, customer, product, and employee—that's essential for compliance and governance concerns. Technologies such as master data management (MDM) are now part of many BI/PM project plans.

Likely future

With spending numbers at record highs, customer interest is burgeoning in many content areas, and with more vendors competing for their slice of the pie, something will have to give. In the next few years, the BI/PM landscape will shift significantly.

All signs point to industry consolidation. The top four best-of-breed vendors have already exceed or are rapidly approaching the $1 billion mark. When emerging competitors from the enterprise application and platform arenas are anywhere from five to one hundred times larger, it will make sense for some firms to combine.

Lots of questions arise, but no clear answers are available yet. Will the big firms start to swallow the smaller ones? Will smaller ones unite to form an independent alternative to enterprise and platform players? Will someone without a strong market position emerge as an acquirer to get into the BI/PM software market in a big way? Today's market will not even look similar to the one a year from now.

Supply Chain Management

PART
FOUR

The supply chain management (SCM) software market grew out of materials requirements planning (MRP) functionality built as an extension to the manufacturing portions of ERP software. The fundamental innovation in early SCM applications was to apply constraint-based planning and optimization techniques to factory planning and scheduling problems. As corporate users began to demand solutions to broader sets of supply chain problems, the SCM applications category commensurately expanded outside the four walls of the factory. Specialized applications emerged to solve demand planning, transportation and logistics optimization, warehouse management, and multi-echelon inventory optimization issues. To distinguish themselves, vendors have since increasingly tailored their planning products to specific industry problems, applying techniques such as constraint-based optimization, stochastic optimization, genetic algorithms, neural networks, and advanced statistical modeling and optimization to address distinct network planning needs.

The SCM market first started to coalesce in the mid to late 1990s. At that time, Manugistics and i2 Technologies emerged as two of the leading providers of supply chain planning application suites. In the late 1990s, SAP and Oracle, among others, began to aggressively pursue the SCM opportunity, initially through internal development of their own SCM suite of products. In 2001, after over promising the value of SCM applications, the SCM market began to falter. Many electronic marketplaces with poor business models failed, and buying companies recoiled from the overselling. Today's market is characterized by a buying community that recognizes and needs the business value these applications can provide, but is also more practical in its expectations.

ERP vendors increasingly play a large role in this market, but the leading companies are either pushing the limits of best-of-breed products through joint development work or are building their own applications internally or though partners. They are using existing mature application components mixed with innovative custom abilities in the form of composite applications.

Market size and growth rates

The SCM market reached about $5.5 billion in total market size and is expected to grow 7 percent in 2006. Consolidation will continue to play a major role in the SCM market.

Key players

The SCM applications market is more fragmented than many other application segments. The five largest vendors by revenue share—SAP, Oracle, i2, Manhattan Associates, and IBS—make up a combined 31 percent of the total revenue of the SCM applications market. SAP and Oracle have shown the largest market share gains in the past few years—SAP by growing organically and building a dense partner ecosystem on top of its NetWeaver platform, and Oracle through organic growth and an aggressive acquisition strategy that included the supply chain assets of PeopleSoft, JD Edwards, Retek, G-Log, and Demantra, with more likely to be announced soon.

Company Name	Revenue, 2004 ($M)	Revenue, 2005 ($M)	Revenue Forecast, 2006 ($M)	Revenue Share, 2004	Revenue Share, 2005	Revenue Share Forecast, 2006	Growth Rate, 2004-2005	Growth Rate Forecast, 2005-2006
SAP	619	654	706	11%	12%	12%	6%	8%
Oracle	288	568	585	5%	10%	10%	97%	3%
i2 Technologies	297	276	260	5%	5%	4%	-7%	-6%
Manhattan Associates	215	246	270	4%	4%	4%	15%	10%
Infor	97	192	231	2%	3%	4%	98%	20%
IBS	191	185	191	3%	3%	3%	-3%	3%
Manugistics	187	160	144	3%	3%	2%	-15%	-10%
Swisslog	128	128	128	2%	2%	2%	0%	0%
RedPrairie	122	127	170	2%	2%	3%	4%	34%
Activant	92	96	97	2%	2%	2%	4%	1%
Subtotal	2236	2633	2782	41%	47%	46%	18%	6%
Total SCM Market	5473	5637	6013	100%	100%	100%	3%	7%

—— Top ten SCM vendors ranked by 2005 SCM revenue (incl. est. '06 growth)

i2, once the dominant force in the SCM market, has seen its market share fall following a revenue restatement and decline while it restructured in line with new market forces. i2's revenue has stabilized, although at a fraction of its peak, and the company is now working to reestablish a growth trajectory. Meanwhile, Manhattan Associates has been a steady performer, building on its warehouse management roots and making strategic acquisitions, including Logistics.com in transportation management and, more recently, the acquisition of Evant to move into supply chain planning markets.

ERP vendors look to continue consolidating market share gains based on current spending patterns. Innovation, however, continues to come from a large number of industry-targeted startup and emerging software vendors. For many of these innovators, their likely exit will be acquisition by larger SCM suite providers.

Shifts in functionality

Current trends in functionality can be characterized by the following:

- Maturation of core application functionality, unlocking the promise of market value and return on investment

- The promising development of advanced supply and demand planning technologies that push the edges of the applications of statistical and operations research, creating the ability to model and solve complex network problems with substantially better business results

- Flexible multiprotocol platforms for interenterprise planning and coordination

Core applications in areas like demand planning are becoming more standardized, packaged, and widely deployed. At the same time, more advanced demand management applications look to use downstream channel data to provide higher levels of demand insight and demand shaping. Warehouse management and transportation management applications continue to grow in functionality and deliver a tangible benefit, with interest in transportation management surging as of late because of constrained capacity and rising fuel costs.

Environmental factors, such as the rise of global outsourcing and the increasing frequency of new product introductions, are requiring substantially tighter collaboration and coordination across increasingly complex networks of trading partners. As heightened complexity becomes mainstream reality, the ability to manage supply and demand uncertainty becomes an essential competency.

Therefore, some of the most advanced science is being applied in the areas of multi-echelon inventory optimization and service parts planning. The main value is the ability to model and solve multitier, time-phased problems that recommend inventory levels and replenishment policies at each level of a multitier network. This, in turn, increases the probability of attaining desired service levels or fill rates with less total inventory investment. Similarly, software is now emerging to support the more strategic problems of asset allocation and network design. Supply chain planning software vendors are developing optimization techniques as well as collaboration and integration frameworks to help support planning and collaboration between trading partners. Finally, companies are seeing great benefit from merging analytics with optimization. This creates closed-loop decision making for critical processes like demand management, inventory optimization, and sales and operations planning (S&OP).

Current and emerging business models

The dominant business model in SCM is similar to most other enterprise application segments. Customers typically license software on a perpetual license basis, contract for implementation services on top of the license cost, and pay an ongoing maintenance fee of 15 to 20 percent to secure support from their vendor and to fund application enhancements.

The notable shift in the SCM market is from a high-growth segment—with an average revenue mix of 50 to 60 percent license revenue, 20 to 30 percent services revenue, and 15 to 20 percent maintenance—to a market in which services and maintenance are the major sources of revenue. The reasons for this shift are that, for starters, companies rebelled against the increasingly high license fees being charged from 1998 to the crash in 2001. Secondly, they recognized that SCM projects require a significant level of change management, business process redesign, and data- and process-level integration, which in turn require a larger services component. SCM applications, especially the advanced optimizers, are increasingly not packaged applications, but powerful toolsets that require careful implementation to meet the business goals of the corporation.

Two other important shifts are also underway:

- Companies are increasingly contracting for their SCM applications on a subscription basis rather than on a perpetual license basis. They are doing this to avoid large, upfront license payment in favor of a model that spreads cost over a longer period.

- Software as a service is gaining momentum. While the adoption of SaaS in SCM has trailed the uptake in areas like customer management or supply management markets, SaaS is starting to take hold in some areas, like transportation and global trade management. It will continue to grow as a deployment and delivery option for companies.

Impact of new technology

Service-oriented architectures are an increasingly important technology development. SCM application providers were early adopters of SOA because of the high rate of customization in implementations and the need to use data from numerous existing applications and legacy data sources. Many SCM applications are parasitic in nature, requiring data from many external sources to provide decision support outcomes. This trend will continue, since most vendors have either already converted, or are in the process of converting, their applications to the new flexible architecture.

Beyond the data integration aspect, the follow-on effect of moving to SOA and componentizing applications is to make SCM components more easily available as services within composite application frameworks. As a result, innovative companies are capitalizing on maturing SOA, business process management, and workflow technologies to create customized composite applications.

The need for multicompany, multitier visibility has also led to investment in connectivity technologies as well as the creation of hubs such as E2open and Exostar. This goes beyond pure connectivity and visibility to support multitier collaboration. To create more effective multiparty scenario planning, vendors such as Kinaxis are building tactical order and inventory management products that use forecast, inventory, order, capacity, and logistics data from heterogeneous ERP and SCM applications. This new set of applications represents a fundamental change in SCM applications toward buy- and sell-side, service-level-based commerce and away from transactional interactions.

Likely future

The SCM market will change significantly along two dimensions. First, the definition of supply chain management will continue to expand, blurring the lines separating SCM from other application categories. For example, SCM applications are no longer point optimization engines used purely for decision support. Instead, the support of supply chain execution, collaboration, and workflow in the tactical and operational realm (rather than just strategic planning) are increasingly part of the value of these applications. A prime example of this is the growth of vendor-managed inventory (VMI) and supplier-managed inventory (SMI), SMI relationships, and the technology to support them. SCM applications are also increasingly important to the success of processes not always considered part of the pure SCM realm, like new product development and introduction (NPDI). Beyond the design, product lifecycle management, and sourcing components, companies need to support complex planning and collaboration, thus boosting NPDI's importance.

The second dimension is the vendor landscape. As the SCM market matures, the number of large successful vendors will inevitably consolidate. ERP vendors like Oracle and Infor are leading the consolidation. Suite vendors like i2, Manhattan Associates, and JDA Software may become more active in the acquisition market, as well.

Supply Management: Procurement and Sourcing

The supply management market is made up of a combination of procurement, sourcing, contract management, and supplier performance management (SPM) suites. Typically transaction/execution-oriented procurement applications include procure to pay, catalog, and supplier on-boarding functionality. Sourcing applications (spend analytics, RFX, e-negotiation, and auctions) and contract management are an integral part of the toolset for executing supply management strategies. SPM includes supplier scorecard, dashboard, alert messaging, and supplier assessment capabilities.

Since the 1990s, procurement applications have provided companies with the ability to streamline the procurement transactions from requisition to order to pay. This functionality, originally offered as point applications to existing ERP applications, has advanced tremendously. The point applications have grown to suites, nonvalue-add activities are now automated, and strategic supply management functionality has been added to the suite offerings.

Market size and growth rates

In 2005, the procurement and sourcing market grew by 10 percent and is now a $2.2 billion market. We forecast this market will continue with similar growth next year. Most of it is attributed to the typical back-office function of procurement/purchasing becoming more strategic to the C-level of the organization. With this elevation, applications need to be easy to use and deploy, and have low risk and low upfront costs. For many, software as a service addresses these concerns.

Expect some consolidation in the industry. Watch for partnerships that may lead to mergers and acquisitions among the point product vendors, particularly in the settlement and supply network areas. We also expect to see procurement-and-sourcing-specific point products partner up with each other (such as procurement with sourcing) to broaden a current system into a suite.

Key players

SAP, Ariba, and Oracle are today's market leaders of the 70 vendors that participate in the category. In 2005, the three leaders were joined by an additional eight that grew 10 percent year over year: AT Kearney, Emptoris, ePlus, IBS, ICG Commerce, Perfect Commerce, Procuri, and Silver Oak Solutions. Watch for the ERP vendors' continued strengthening of supplier relationship management (SRM) hosting in 2006.

In addition, retail-specific sourcing vendors are also hitting the market. Eqos, ecVision, Freeborders, Jesta, NGC, Tourtellotte Solutions, Tradestone, and Zymmetry round out typical e-negotiation tools with various levels of purchase order, collaboration tracking, and product lifecycle management (PLM) functionality.

Shifts in functionality

When procurement systems emerged in the 1990s, they typically only addressed the workflow approval process, with some online catalog functionality, as well. It now includes procure-to-pay processes, full workflow, and catalog and supplier on-boarding. The procurement purchase cycle of requisition-order-receipt-pay for in-

Company Name	Revenue, 2004 ($M)	Revenue, 2005 ($M)	Revenue Forecast, 2006 ($M)	Revenue Share, 2004	Revenue Share, 2005	Revenue Share Forecast, 2006	Growth Rate, 2004-2005	Growth Rate Forecast, 2005-2006
SAP	300	337	381	15%	15%	16%	12%	13%
Ariba	280	312	323	14%	14%	14%	12%	3%
Oracle	131	258	297	7%	12%	12%	98%	15%
AT Kearney	44	60	69	2%	3%	3%	38%	15%
Lawson	57	55	65	3%	3%	3%	-4%	18%
Silver Oak Solutions	20	45	0	1%	2%	0%	125%	-100%
Dun & Bradstreet	42	42	45	2%	2%	2%	0%	5%
ICG Commerce	33	38	48	2%	2%	2%	14%	26%
IBS	32	37	39	2%	2%	2%	16%	5%
i2 Technologies	36	34	37	2%	2%	2%	-7%	10%
Subtotal	975	1219	1304	58%	63%	63%	25%	7%
Total Procurement and Sourcing Market	1991	2181	2381	100%	100%	100%	10%	9%

—— Top ten procurement and sourcing vendors ranked by 2005 procurement and sourcing revenue (incl. est. '06 growth)

181

direct spending is now complete. Direct materials and maintenance, repair, and overhaul (MRO) functions have been added where applicable. The last spend segment to be added was business services, as enhancements in labor costs and invoicing took some time.

With greater transaction automation, the shift to strategic supply management has been natural. Sourcing applications introduced in the late 1990s brought e-negotiations, RFX, and auction functionality. Customers quickly found they could streamline the quote, analysis, and award process, and with it came huge savings from the visible competition. But customers were still looking for additional savings and to reduce the time from award to contract. The addition of project management, contract, and spend analysis applications has helped streamline this workflow over the past few years. Sourcing systems are now suites of applications that have leaned out the business process.

AMR Research expects to see greater emphasis on supplier performance management as companies move from just managing supplier relationships to managing their performance in the context of each firm's business requirements. Companies that have improved their supply management function are now looking to streamline performance management and tie it back to spending, commodity councils, and strategies.

Current and emerging business models

The current business model in the procurement and sourcing segment has not changed much since this market's inception. Most vendors sell their own products through a combination of direct sales representatives and service providers. The vast majority of customer purchases have been perpetual software licenses based primarily on the number of users. Maintenance fees, which cover support and product enhancements, typically cost 16 to 20 percent of the net license fees. In most cases, the necessary IT infrastructure (middleware, hardware, and networking) is sold by the software vendor or technology partner. The consulting and implementation services are provided by some combination of the software vendor and service provider.

We do expect some changes to the procurement and sourcing business models in the next few years:

- The vendors will focus more on small and midsize businesses, moving the procurement and sourcing application market to become more volume driven.

- Vendors will continue to look for greater opportunities in the Asian-Pacific, Latin American, and European markets. Watch for vendors to expand their products through partnerships or mergers. Language and currency functionality will separate products from localized to global.

- SaaS will continue to grow as an option. The growth will ensure that procurement and sourcing, hosting, and managed services will become even more prevalent. Expect increased competition, however, as ERP vendors enhance their SRM functionality using SaaS.

- As the application revenue model changes to SaaS, vendors will broaden their services to include business process out-sourcing (BPO) as a segment of their business models.

Impact of new technology

More procurement and sourcing vendors will continue to offer on-demand functionality. It provides faster deployment cycles, is easy to use, and has low upfront costs compared to a licensed model. We expect the momentum in the SaaS market to continue from its phenomenal growth of 125 percent in 2005. Look for greater competition among the SaaS players, with more products in the suites and greater functionality over the next few years.

Licensed applications will continue to decline, but they won't completely go away. Vendors will continue to increase their consulting and services segments to make up for the difference in the revenue model and pricing models of licenses and SaaS.

Likely future

The procurement and sourcing market will continue to grow 9 to 10 percent each year for the next few years. We anticipate this market segment will experience a CAGR of 8 percent through 2010.

The market will expand in three ways:

- Greater dependency on BPO
- Increased services
- Expanded product/service functionality

The BPO market will grow based on board-level decisions to move the management of transactions that previously had been back-room functions to the C-level for complete cost control. The change will happen in steps, starting with either outsourced procurement or sourcing, and then moving to the other over time. From a sourcing perspective, indirect areas will be outsourced first because most companies will keep their core products in house.

Services will expand to include low-cost country sourcing initiatives, BPO and sourcing commodity, and event assistance.

Functionality additions will include the following:

- Supply visibility with advanced shipping notices (ASNs) and inventory replenishment
- Integrated supply management suites that cover all areas of spend: direct, indirect, services, and MRO
- Supplier portal technology
- Collaboration tracking
- PLM lite
- Supplier risk management as a standard in SPM
- Supplier networks
- "Should be" and "new" cost modeling
- Sourcing marriage of the physical and financial flow
- Settlement activity

Customer Relationship Management

Customer relationship management (CRM), and the broader customer management applications market, has reemerged as one of the fastest-growing enterprise application markets. CRM was originally built as a specialized customer master that handled the front-office management of customer-oriented business processes not well addressed by ERP applications at the time. CRM, which can generally be described as the system of record for sales, customer service, and marketing organizations, typically contains discrete modules to address each of these departments. This includes sales force automation (SFA), marketing automation, customer service, contact center, as well as a supporting layer of customer analytics and reporting.

As customer centricity became a major theme for many companies, particularly for service industries like telecommunications and financial services, the CRM market flourished. In 2000, though, CRM suite vendors began to dramatically consolidate, primarily being subsumed into the ERP market. But with renewed interest in revenue and profitability management across industries, there was new demand for the products, which has spawned a second wave of venture-funded customer management startups. The advent of software as a service has created a platform to allow small vendors to create and distribute CRM add-on functionality at an unprecedented pace.

Market size and growth rates

The customer management application market generated nearly $12 billion in total revenue in 2005. Despite one of the largest acquisitions—Oracle buying Siebel—in the CRM market closing in 2006, we expect the total market to continue to grow at 10 percent in 2006. Although demand for customer management applications is increasing across demographics, much of the highest growth is because of hosted SaaS vendors that are selling to small and midsize businesses and increasingly to larger enterprises, as well.

Key players

By the end of 2006, SAP and Oracle (with its acquisition of Siebel) will account for nearly a third of the total customer management applications revenue. Each company's established ERP installed base within large global enterprises will lead to the continued rationalization of CRM products on an incumbent ERP suite. While both vendors attempt to attract new CRM growth within the SMB market, the traditional SMB vendors, such as Microsoft, continue to move upstream to the larger enterprises. Likewise, salesforce.com and RightNow are growing at a torrid pace with their SaaS delivery model, helping lead to more thousand-seat deals in larger enterprises.

Shifts in functionality

The functionality footprints of the standalone CRM vendors were the keys to the success and, in some cases, to the demise of the market leading up to the consolidation of the past few years. While vendors like Siebel became increasingly sophisticated, reports of poor user adoption and lackluster returns on CRM investments grabbed headlines in the early 2000s. Sales and marketing departments, in particular, all too frequently reverted to their faithful spreadsheets and e-mail rather than CRM as their tools of the trade.

Company Name	Revenue, 2004 ($M)	Revenue, 2005 ($M)	Revenue Forecast, 2006 ($M)	Revenue Share, 2004	Revenue Share, 2005	Revenue Share Forecast, 2006	Growth Rate, 2004-2005	Growth Rate Forecast, 2005-2006
SAP	1612	1908	2252	15%	16%	18%	18%	18%
Siebel	1299	1403	0	12%	12%	0%	8%	-100%
Oracle	392	465	1785	4%	4%	14%	19%	284%
amdocs	369	424	487	3%	4%	4%	15%	15%
Dendrite	311	341	352	3%	3%	3%	10%	3%
salesforce.com	176	310	471	2%	3%	4%	76%	52%
Microsoft	202	232	274	2%	2%	2%	15%	18%
RightNow	62	87	170	1%	1%	1%	41%	95%
Subtotal	4423	5170	5791	41%	44%	45%	17%	12%
Total CRM Market	10902	11720	12892	100%	100%	100%	8%	10%

—— Customer management suite vendors ranked by 2005 customer management revenue (incl. est. '06 growth)

187

Over the past several years, CRM vendors have come to recognize that usability and tight desktop tool integration is vital to the success of most implementations. During this time, the emergence of service-oriented architectures and browser-based user interfaces have allowed vendors to create more specialized, integrated, and easier to use applications to help improve adoption rates. A host of new software vendors is also emerging to provide smaller add-on applications that produce ancillary value either from a niche functionality or industry standpoint. As a result, CRM applications have generally become both richer and easier to use.

Current and emerging business models

The traditional business model for CRM suites included a server license and a per-user license component. Like ERP, maintenance fees that cover customer support and upgrades were sold as a percentage of the license cost. Most of the larger CRM vendors' sales were influenced heavily by the specialized CRM practices within the large consulting firms. Although sales, service, and marketing departments were typical users of the software and influenced the buying decisions, it was the IT organization that most often made them. The license model for CRM changed little when it was absorbed into the ERP market. However, consulting organizations now exert less influence because IT departments are most often inclined to consolidate on a single vendor.

Then came SaaS, which has shifted how CRM is paid for and deployed. Blazing the SaaS trail, salesforce.com popularized the multitenancy hosted CRM application in which customers pay a monthly user-based service fee for the use of the application. This fee includes all upgrades and basic customer support, and is typically sold in annual contracts. As a renewal business model, customer service is now paramount in CRM applications, since SaaS vendors need to secure a renewal at the end of each contract. In this model, unused seats turn into lost customers, not just shelfware. As a result of its popularity, most of the large on-premises CRM vendors have built products or strategies for a SaaS model. However, the ways that software companies build, maintain, and support SaaS applications require a very different model than on-premises software, and it is unclear whether any of the established vendors can successfully make this shift.

Impact of new technology

Many of the CRM vendors have shifted from strictly providing business process functionality to adding infrastructure and platforms. Because CRM is usually tightly integrated to back-end systems like ERP, packaged integration points and SOA have become top priorities for most vendors. Large organizations usually have multiple CRM suites and customer management applications in use, mainly because of mergers and acquisitions. As a result, customer data integration (CDI) has become an important technology to help companies build a central, global view of the customer across disparate CRM systems. For large ERP suite vendors, SOA and CDI will help to integrate CRM into their larger application suites more effectively. For the remaining standalone CRM vendors, these integration technologies help reduce the complexity of introducing another vendor into the IT portfolio.

Hosted application architectures have also become a top priority. With hosted CRM seeing a 25 percent CAGR, SaaS has clearly become a viable delivery model for companies of all sizes. As it gains a larger share relative to the licensed CRM software market, customer management software vendors will need a sound strategy to compete. More importantly to smaller private vendors, a good SaaS business model is virtually a prerequisite to attract new venture funding.

Software vendors are also rethinking existing architectures to aid a potential shift to the SaaS delivery model. True SaaS requires that the provider provision service to multiple customers over a single instance of the software to gain true benefits of scale. But the traditional on-premises vendors are finding ways to create hybrid architectures where existing code can be served as a service without rewriting the applications from scratch. They are also repurposing existing data models so that customers can more easily migrate from SaaS to an on-premises deployment.

Likely future

With many different business and technology models in place and more continuing to emerge, customer needs and expectations are changing. The emergence of SaaS is shifting the power to the business buyer, where sales and marketing organizations are often making purchasing decisions largely without IT involvement. At the same time, IT organizations are struggling to rationalize a single vendor for all their enterprise applications. At some point, these two trends will clash, but the business buyer being closer to the revenue will begin to win more of these battles.

As SOA becomes more prevalent for internal application integration, it will better aid the incorporation of SaaS applications for highly specialized or industry-specific business needs, as well. Over the long term, both IT organizations and software vendors will learn how on-premises and SaaS will work together, whether from the same vendor or multiple vendors.

Service Lifecycle Management

Aftermarket services are a business model in which services to fix, maintain, and optimize products are sold to installed bases. Perhaps most importantly, it is the piece of the operation that lets companies understand customer needs and exceed expectations. They use service lifecycle management (SLM) applications to achieve this functionality.

The concept of servicing an installed base is vast, spanning multiple technologies and business processes, including customer management, product development, and supply chain management, among others. In practice, the competency can range from break-and-fix models in the most basic form to performance-based contracts, where long life assets, such as aircraft flight hours, are offered as services.

AMR Research divides SLM into four categories:

- Service discovery—The way companies manage service requests is changing. While some can claim that they proactively assess needs, most are simply reactive and ignore the opportunities. Many only address the identification of service needs when a product breaks and customers call for support.

Rather than responding to problems, service should be proactive, anticipating the needs of customers. The use of condition-monitoring equipment placed in manufacturing sites is an example. By taking constant readings on heat, vibration, noise, and other factors, vendors can understand if there is a problem before equipment fails.

- Service fulfillment—Good service is crucial to the brand. It is the place where consistent opportunity arises to define further sales opportunities, understand customer needs, and exceed customer expectations. Well-integrated systems allow companies to manage scheduling, dispatch people, manage parts availability, and arm technicians with the accurate and timely information that is stored in the knowledge repository.

- Service knowledge—Vital to meeting and exceeding customer expectations is access to installed base and product information. This repository should capture and provide all information to respond to questions quickly and intelligently, while also assessing needs proactively. Often this information is stored within an existing CRM system, but it's far more than a customer contact and sales portal. This knowledge repository also needs to capture and supply repair information, warranty and contract entitlements, and compliance information, as well as track service histories.

- Business management—Here's some basic business math: revenue − expenses = profit. And this is what's wrong with many companies' services strategies: they have no knowledge of expenses, and therefore no knowledge of profitability, which leads to ineffective pricing. Even worse, they have little insight into their customer performance, where they are often legally bound. As buying patterns change to offset more risk to suppliers, service-minded businesses need greater insight into service metrics. Companies are looking for ways to measure profitability as well as performance for service-level agreements (SLAs), and also how to increase competitiveness.

Market size and growth rates

The vendor market size for SLM, estimated to be about $4 billion in 2006, comprises aftermarket services, asset management, and MRO—each representing roughly a third. We expect that the aftermarket services and asset management will join together in the next three to five years as the relevant vendors continue to encroach upon each other's space.

We do expect vigorous growth of 16 percent through 2010 in this market as companies shift from product-based sales to service-based sales. Examples are already prevalent in the A&D, automotive, and industrial equipment industries. A ranking of vendors and their size is not yet possible because most come from other markets, and the size of their SLM revenue is not broken out.

Key players

Three distinct groups of vendors make up the service management space: enterprise software companies, service management vendors, and niche functionality players.

With significant insights and control of transactional data in their manufacturing clients, enterprise application companies such as Oracle, SAP, IFS, and Lawson offer asset management and service functionality. Their value is helping to integrate the extremely diverse nature of managing a client's service needs, from managing the incoming call to field service, parts requisitioning, entitlement management, and contract management.

The main service management suite vendors include Astea, Click Commerce, ClickSoftware, Indus, MCA Solutions, Metrix, ServiceBench, Servigistics, and Vertical Solutions. These companies are evolving into this space, each with unique attributes for customer management, field service execution, decision support, or parts management. These products integrate with existing enterprise systems, often competing with the incumbent enterprise vendor for these value-added services.

Niche functionality vendors usually partner with the previously mentioned companies or are deployed extremely narrowly to address a given pain point. Examples include products to provide technicians with mobile functionality, tools to assess new product failure rates, and logistics tools.

Vendor	Headquarters	Company Revenue
Astea	Horsham, PA	$10M–$100M
Click Commerce	Chicago, IL	$10M–$100M
ClickSoftware	Burlington, MA	$10M–$100M
IFS	Linköping, Sweden	$100M–$1B
Indus	Atlanta, GA	$100M–$1B
Lawson	St. Paul, MN	$100M–$1B
Metrix	Waukesha, WI	Less Than $10M
Oracle–E-Business Suite	Redwood Shores, CA	More Than $1B
Oracle–JD Edwards	Redwood Shores, CA	More Than $1B
Oracle–PeopleSoft	Redwood Shores, CA	More Than $1B
Oracle–Siebel	Redwood Shores, CA	More Than $1B
SAP	Walldorf, Germany	More Than $1B
ServiceBench	Fairfax, VA	Less Than $10M
ServicePower	Stockport, England	$10M–$100M
Servigistics	Atlanta, GA	$10M–$100M
Vertical Solutions	Cincinnati, OH	$10M–$100M

SLM vendors—general information

Shifts in functionality

The large enterprise application companies have long been in control of manufacturing and customer data. They then grew into the service space to expand their reach into the businesses of clients. They began offering a host of modular products aimed at responding to end-customer needs, such as call center management, order management, and contract management. Soon this evolved into scheduling and dispatch and parts management, ultimately culminating in service-oriented suites that are capable of managing large installations, such as oil rigs and manufacturing plants. The aim of many of these earlier systems was to make the service groups as efficient as possible and reduce costs.

Maintenance of large-scale industrial equipment has traditionally been provided by a combination of equipment vendor and local facility maintenance and engineering personnel. However, as the maintenance ranks dwindle because of attrition and retirement, manufacturers are increasingly dependent on outsourced maintenance providers or on the equipment suppliers themselves. This has opened up a new services market opportunity for equipment providers, many of which have developed new business models, offering multiyear asset maintenance and asset performance management service agreements to their manufacturing clients. This shift from asset maintenance as an internal cost burden to asset maintenance as a business has created new software support requirements and modern asset management software, which typically includes help desk, customer call center, and workforce dispatch.

Acknowledging this budding market, service-oriented suites were created that offered best-of-breed functionality to customers that did not choose to further rely on deployed enterprise software. These suites often have an industry focus and are relatively quickly deployed.

One of the major factors in service cost and repair time is the management of service parts, with analysis tools currently moving from niche to mainstream functionality. Software-based mathematical models are being used to support some key functions, like determining optimum network design, calculating the mean time between part failures, and optimizing the tradeoff between maximizing service levels and inventory investment. This type of decision support is helping rearchitect network and distribution models, while also feeding critical information for preventive maintenance and even product design.

Current and emerging business models

Aftermarket services are becoming a major profit center for many companies, and application vendors are looking to meet the growing needs. Here are some cross-industry samples:

- Expensive, long-life assets, such as aircraft engines and construction equipment, are historically sold at low margins, but with lucrative service contracts. Perhaps product should be considered a loss leader as a way to sell more predictable and profitable service contracts.

- Fixing late-model vehicles often requires specialty tools, and thus a trip to the dealer. Independent and franchise automotive shops often have trouble competing in time, quality, and price. Designing proprietary components can help lock in customers to use your service rather than going with a third party.

- Premium chain hotels are famous for noting clientele preferences and duplicating their (sometimes eccentric) wishes as they stay throughout the world. This attention to detail enhances brand and increases repeat business while fostering extremely profitable rates. Staying close to the customer and personalizing service helps create artificial walls between you and competitors, increasing the probability of repeat purchases.

- Big-box retail stores are investing in their service groups. After years of successfully selling service contracts, retailers are now investing in field service to build customer intimacy and create incremental profits.

In response to these opportunities, vendors are looking to build up suites, and acquisitions have been plentiful. We expect acquisitions to continue as the smaller companies look to build best-of-breed suites to battle the enterprise player's scale and dominance.

Impact of new technology

Aftermarket services are complex, spanning multiple corporate divisions, partners, geographies, and technologies. As such, customers are requesting that vendors rebuild their systems based on an SOA strategy. This should make it easier for customers to configure, deploy, and manage their systems. It should also help them respond more quickly to market and process changes.

Likely future

Demand-driven supply networks (DDSNs) are often discussed in relation to consumer products, but sensing and responding to demand signals is a tremendous opportunity for post-sales services, as well. Evolutionary and revolutionary business models are creating competitive advantages for companies that can proactively anticipate, understand, and address user needs, ultimately leading to increased profits and customer loyalty.

The culmination of these endeavors is the ability to offer performance-based services, where performance can be defined as availability, quality, satisfaction, customer experience, or a variety of other factors. A few key areas are needed to build to this level of competency:

- Design for service—Profitable service begins with creating products that are designed with specific features to aid the technician. Examples include replacing assemblies rather than fixing small components, and locking mechanisms rather than using screws. Most importantly, it means detailed and accurate repair information and timely service bulletins in the hands of technicians when they need it.

- Service parts management—To profitably deliver service and fulfill the customer's need for uptime or performance, excellent service parts management is critical. Understanding the various levels of criticality of certain parts to product uptime and balancing the tradeoff between service levels and the service parts inventory budget are extremely valuable but challenging propositions. The organizations that have implemented the tools and expertise to support new service models actively simulate, model, and test their planning assumptions and outputs.

- Network design—Designing the network for serviceability is also vital. Considerations include where to place part-stocking locations and repair depots and how many facilities and locations to have, not to mention examining whether the right field service engineers have the right parts and expertise to deliver service within the service level promised. One high-tech company has a control-room view of its service network. As it signs new customers, it can evaluate if it has the right assets to meet the promised service level to the customer, or if it needs to add capacity or change the terms of the SLA.

- Profitably pricing services—While products in the field have service history, new products have little data on common failures, costs to remedy, and ultimate performance. Mastering this competency is the difference between extremely lucrative, high-profile deals and financial disaster.

B2B E-Business

In the broadest terms, B2B e-business is any form of computer-assisted communication between trading partners. AMR Research defines it as the digitization of a broad range of interactions among trading partners, including orders, plans, logistics, settlement, design, quality, and performance management. It is evolving from simple messaging to include shared multi-enterprise services for visibility, collaboration, and automated response to changing conditions.

While the revenue for the segment is still dominated by the traditional electronic data interchange (EDI) value-added networks (VANs), its boundaries are blurring as the functions are subsumed into broader managed services, trading exchanges, and middleware providers.

As a result, companies can approach their trading partner communication needs from a variety of angles, with most using a combination of complementary and even competing products and services.

Market size and growth rates

Reliable information on this market is scarce because many of the largest players have been acquired by private capital or telecommunications companies. The remainder are either emerging or niche companies or target small and midsize businesses. We conservatively estimate this market at $1.8 billion. 59 percent of this is traditional EDI VANs, managed file transfer, and other messaging services— ones that have long dominated the market. We expect growth of about 3 percent as traditional VAN services continue their slow decline, being replaced by other forms of messaging, such as AS2. New forms of services will take their place, accounting for the bulk of the growth, with a little help from software products for translation and integration.

Key players

Companies that get the bulk of their revenue through providing traditional VAN services still dominate, holding 75 percent of the B2B e-business market. Software vendors hold 15 percent, and managed services or SaaS hold 10 percent. Sterling Commerce, GXS, Inovis, and Axway are rapidly trying to reinvent themselves with new services, accounting for the difference between VAN services spending (59 percent) and this total. EasyLink Services trails this list as it fights a rearguard action against the decline of the VAN.

SEEBURGER and webMethods are playing significant roles as e-business software providers, targeting the integration and business process needs of e-business, while E2open is the leader of the emerging hub market. These vendors and a host of smaller ones play a major role filling in the gaps left by SAP and Oracle, which lack significant capabilities in the core messaging part of the market.

Shifts in functionality

Like most other industries, consolidation and footprint expansion are the norm. In many cases, the survivors of the B2B Internet bubble are reassembling to offer a broader range of services aimed at specific industries:

- Sterling Commerce consolidated Yantra, TR2, and Nistevo to break out of the VAN business and launch multi-enterprise supply chain services for retailers.

- Axway acquired Cyclone Commerce to build a platform for distributed supply chain tracking services.

- E2open acquired GetSilicon to expand its coverage to manufacturing applications from just supply chain.

- Descartes has evolved somewhat differently from the VANs, providing visibility services. It then acquired VAN and additional SaaS companies to provide a more complete supply chain visibility and collaboration environment, primarily focusing on the global movement of goods.

These applications are at the forefront of new demand-driven strategies, which are inherently multi-enterprise in nature. The services are more likely to come in the form of an Internet-based application, with a combination of messaging and role-specific user interfaces to solve a particular business problem. These extended supply chain problems are specialized enough that the vendors are usually targeting specific industries, such as retail or electronics.

Current and emerging business models

The diversity of the B2B market and the convergence on a technology-supported managed services model makes it difficult to characterize. Things as different as Ariba's procurement services and webMethods' enterprise application integration (EAI)/business process management (BPM) software are providing connections between trading partners. Companies that were once categorized together, such as VANs or trading exchanges, are playing in the same B2B market.

The broader change, however, is happening in the business models where companies are shifting from software or messaging services to managed services supporting specific business processes. Unlike the inward-facing functionality of most enterprise applications, the B2B market's one-to-one message is changing to a new world of applications shared over multiple business partners in a supply network. Consider the following:

- The messaging and translator space is blurring, with EAI and BPM starting to overlap, especially as SEEBURGER seeks to displace webMethods as the preferred vendor in SAP accounts.

- The traditional VANs are moving up market to provide supply chain applications as well as messaging services.

- E2open, Hubspan, and i2 (the RiverOne acquisition) are examples of second generation e-business hubs with a range of communication methods (e-mail, web, EDI, and XML messaging) to meet the varied sizes and abilities of trading partners. They also made higher level supply chain visibility, shared planning, and shared metrics a core part of the value proposition. Adding specific support for business processes, such as vendor-managed inventory, in a multitenant hub, they became examples of SaaS.

- The surviving trading exchanges from the early 1990s are primarily industry consortia that were never shutdown, like the venture-funded companies. Though they will never pay back the millions invested in them, they carved out a niche by creating shared platforms for e-business that reduce costs in an industry for business processes that don't provide any one player a competitive advantage.

All the companies (except for the software pure plays) are moving toward the managed services area. They are more than SaaS, but not quite business process outsourcers. However, they facilitate a business process on their platform, and may act on the principal's behalf in executing it. This requires specific expertise to offer additional business services and escape the commodity trap of the VAN or trading exchange world.

The most successful in using this managed services approach has been the e-procurement vendors, such as Ariba and Perfect Commerce. They host analytics and sourcing software and facilitate sourcing events, such as auctions. They also have commodity experts to help develop bidding documents. (Though they do offer supplier communication services, we did not include them in the market sizing).

The former VANs and trading exchanges are scrambling to add these types of services for procurement and supply chain. Their advantage over enterprise vendors, such as SAP and Oracle, will be to create a shared universe or hub for multiple supply network partners independent of each company's inward-focused ERP system.

Impact of new technology

The glacial pace of industry standards has been slowing the market for years, especially the raft of XML-based standards that started during the e-business bubble. While enormous amounts of work have been done by leading adopters, mass adoption by smaller companies never seems to come closer. They stick to traditional EDI, use portals, or invest in whatever one-off integration their partner demands. This won't change anytime soon unless forced by a major retailer or industry mandate. If a simpler, cheaper way exists to get the job done, even the cheerleaders will face pressure within their own companies to use it.

At its heart, B2B e-business is still an integration problem. The new emphasis in business processes will make it a testing ground for emerging SOA-based products. For example, the shared hub need not be just a portal or a place to upload files like today, but could actively include each company's ERP system in a shared business process. The technology will allow the hub provider to create an innovative, multicompany business process without requiring changes to the underlying enterprise applications. This may serve to further slow upgrades of ERP, as companies can live with slow-changing core processes and innovate on the outside.

Likely future

Basic communications are becoming commoditized and subsumed by larger offerings, effectively ceasing to be separately priced. Watch for continued experimentation in business models as different vendors try to determine the best combination of services and functionality.

The big question will be how far they stray into the BPO space. As brand owners trying to manage an extended global supply chain have found, there are no arm's length relationships. Trading partners and service providers have to work out a mutually profitable division of responsibilities to create the next generation of shared B2B e-business applications.

Product Lifecycle Management

PART
NINE

The product lifecycle management (PLM) market, first defined by AMR Research in 1999, is a business process and technology strategy for the creation and support of the product knowledge necessary to design, manufacture, and support a compliant product across its lifecycle. Typical lifecycle processes supported include cross-functional new product development, manufacturing process planning, continuous product improvement, and service documentation.

PLM grew out of the need to expand access to a previously engineering-centric product data management (PDM) system to a broader group of people across an extended enterprise and supply chain. It has since expanded to include five core components: PDM, collaborative product-process design (CPD), direct material sourcing (DMS), customer needs management (CNM), and product portfolio management (PPM).

Market size and growth rates

The 2005 PLM market reached $10.5 billion, with a growth of 9 percent. It is expected to reach $11.3 billion in 2006, with a five-year CAGR of 9 percent growing to $16 billion by 2010. The non-CAD portion represented a 45 percent share and grew slightly faster at 11 percent CAGR. CPD captured the top 2005 revenue share at 20 percent and had the highest growth rate at 16 percent.

Key players

The top PLM vendors derive from either a computer-aided design (CAD) or ERP background, with neutral applications in the market as well.

- CAD vendor Dassault Systemes is also top in PLM revenue, followed by UGS and PTC.

- ERP providers include SAP, which leads in revenue, with Oracle and Baan (Infor) most active from a product direction.

- Agile Software remains the most common of the CAD- and ERP-neutral PLM applications after MatrixOne was acquired by Dassault Systemes in mid-2006.

Shifts in functionality

In 1999, PLM functionality primarily involved extending engineering-centric PDM to the rest of the enterprise through the rising Internet. At that time, one of our surveys indicated improving global visibility of changing product information for the entire product launch team and extending PDM access for immediate value were the main factors behind investment. This then led to the next phase of PLM: adding business process functionality to support different constituents using product information in their daily activities.

Collaboration applications were a natural fit, allowing the cross-functional teams to electronically participate in design reviews. Supply chain and procurement became an immediate opportunity where added DMS allowed these professionals to participate in sourcing decisions early in the design phase to reduce the costs associated

Company Name	Revenue, 2004 ($M)	Revenue, 2005 ($M)	Revenue Forecast, 2006 ($M)	Revenue Share, 2004	Revenue Share, 2005	Revenue Share Forecast, 2006	Growth Rate, 2004-2005	Growth Rate Forecast, 2005-2006
Cadence	1197	1329	1425	12%	13%	13%	11%	7%
Dassault	988	1168	1392	10%	11%	12%	18%	19%
UGS	978	1155	1299	10%	11%	12%	18%	12%
PTC	672	744	818	7%	7%	7%	11%	10%
Mentor Graphics	711	705	755	7%	7%	7%	-1%	7%
SAP	381	380	410	4%	4%	4%	0%	8%
Lectra Systems	284	277	301	3%	3%	3%	-2%	9%
MSC Software	267	296	320	3%	3%	3%	11%	8%
Autodesk	200	257	308	2%	2%	3%	29%	20%
Gerber Technology	154	162	170	2%	2%	2%	5%	5%
Subtotal	5833	6473	7198	60%	61%	64%	11%	11%
Total PLM Market	9658	10536	11277	100%	100%	100%	9%	7%

—Top ten PLM vendors ranked by 2005 PLM revenue (incl. est. '06 growth)

207

with the proliferation of new part numbers and materials. As executives grew frustrated with poor visibility into product development, a demand rose for PPM functionality to better manage the product development pipeline. Manufacturers still need to ensure designs profitably meet customer requirements, which our studies show is one of the primary causes of failed product launches. This is leading to a rising interest in CNM features to improve alignment of the voice of the customer with product design.

While the core components of PLM exist today, the functionality can be extended to support a number of manufacturing process initiatives, including design for manufacture and supply, sensing customer demand, and decision support across the entire product lifecycle. Specific industry needs are still a rich opportunity, such as managing embedded software in a mature PLM industry, like automotive, or managing specifications for a growing industry, like food and beverage.

Current and emerging business models

PLM mirrors much of the enterprise software application market in pricing and distribution strategies. The core model is to sell perpetual software licenses of different modules based on a set of named users, with pricing by concurrent user available to a lesser degree. A software maintenance fee averaging 18 to 22 percent is common, though occasionally vendors will require a license renewal fee to continue using the application. Depending on scope and complexity, implementation services typically run one to three times the cost of the software investment. Vendors typically offer their own implementation services, but rely heavily on third-party system integrators (SIs) to provide business process consulting as well as scale for implementation.

A few new entries into the market are offering access to all product modules for any licensed user. Very few vendors are offering single-instance, multitenant software as a service, with most offering variations of this model that tend to be about creative pricing for hosted applications. The move into the small-to-midsize business market is generating much of this creative pricing, while also leading vendors to package applications and pricing that is attractive to their growing list of channel partners.

208

Impact of new technology

Hardware performance for speed and storage is a constraint for many power users, such as engineers, when designing and collaborating with graphic-intensive files. This has many vendors moving toward 64-bit technology and grid computing. New formats for sharing 3D representations of products in a compressed file format are emerging rapidly, allowing files to be embedded into documents and e-mail messages. Service-oriented architectures are being adopted in varying degrees by vendors as they find they need to interact with other applications that are critical to a successful product launch. This will allow them to subscribe to the disparate information required to support design decisions, and to better participate in an event-driven business process.

Likely future

The non-CAD portion of the PLM market is expected to grow at a double-digit pace over the next five years as manufacturers seek a greater return on product innovation. However, we expect the functionality found within PLM today to better integrate with other business applications to properly support the new product introduction process as well as the full product lifecycle. This will make SOA critical to the future of these applications, and will continue the trend set by companies to base their full PLM strategy on a CAD and/or ERP foundation, capitalizing on the strategic IT investments that have been made. However, there is plenty of room for innovative applications, particularly in the areas of customer needs and decision support. Growth will come from adding capabilities in these areas as well as extending into less mature industries, including consumer packaged goods and apparel.

Manufacturing Operations

Manufacturing operations refers to the set of business processes and activities directly involved with the manufacture of a product. Software applications that serve the needs of this market segment are diverse, often offering functionality that's tailored to the requirements of specific styles and types of manufacturing. Major manufacturing operations software application categories include the following:

- Enterprise manufacturing intelligence (EMI)

- Manufacturing execution systems (MES)

- Enterprise asset management (EAM)

- Data historians

- Product quality management, statistical process control (SPC), quality management systems (QMS), and laboratory information management systems (LIMS)

- Advanced process control (APC) and advanced process simulation (APS)

- Specification management, product data management, and recipe management

- Finite capacity (plant) scheduling
- Batch execution/supervisory control and data acquisition (SCADA) and human-machine interface (HMI)

Most significantly, EMI is an emerging functional category that is of particular interest because it supports geographically dispersed supply network operations (SNO), bridging the gap between ERP and traditional, locally deployed, execution-oriented manufacturing operations applications. SNO refers to the orchestration of manufacturing operations when the fleet of manufacturing sites is globally distributed and blended—a mix of wholly owned and contract manufacturing assets.

Market size and growth rates

The market for manufacturing operations software applications is highly fragmented due to the diversity and complexity of manufacturing processes. This has made it impossible for software vendors to develop configurable products and achieve economies of scale. Consequently, the market is difficult to size because of the sheer number and diversity of vendors and the high proportion of spending on in-house manufacturing software or massive customization of commercial software that's over 65 percent of the manufacturing application software market. We estimate the market for manufacturing operations application software at $5 billion to $7 billion:

- The 2005 market for MES is roughly $1 billion and still growing.
- The 2005 market for EAM applications is just shy of $1 billion.
- The 2005 combined revenue for LIMS, quality management, batch execution, SCADA, APC/APS, and current EMI application segments is approaching $1 billion.

These best-of-breed point products add up to a $3 billion market, without factoring in revenue contributions from ERP applications being used in the production management capacity, which potentially adds an additional $3 billion to this estimate.

AMR Research's annual software application spending studies for 2005 and 2006 show that the perception of manufacturing operations as a strategic software application category has risen dramatically in the past three years. Manufacturing operations and associated application spending are expected to grow strongly through the end of the decade, particularly as manufacturers play catch-up servicing nearly two decades of pent-up demand. The market for manufacturing operations software has the potential to reach between $10 billion and $12 billion by the end of the decade, helped by emerging industrial economies in India and China that are starting to hit their stride, as well as ERP vendors applying their hefty marketing and R&D budgets to capitalize on the rediscovery of manufacturing.

Software Vendor/Application	Percentage of Companies Using
SAP	12%
Oracle (including JD Edwards)	4%
Microsoft	2%
All other	5%
In-house developed applications by internal staff/developers	37%
Custom developed applications by a third-party vendor	30%
Desktop productivity applications	7%

2006 primary software vendor—manufacturing operations

Key players

The manufacturing operations application landscape is character-ized by the notable absence of large dominant players. Instead, the landscape is segmented among the following:

- Large automation vendors—ABB, Emerson, GE Fanuc, Honeywell, Invensys, Rockwell, and Siemens offer software to augment their automation and controls products. However, their software revenue is insignificant next to the greater than $100 billion in revenue for their automation and controls. These titans of manufacturing have struggled to translate their manufacturing know-how into leadership in the manufactur-ing operations software category.

- Small best-of-breed vendors—Numerous vendors, most with $20 million or less in revenue, are addressing EMI, MES, EAM, QMS, APC/APS, batch recipe execution, and histori-ans, as well as a host of highly specialized applications. These niche software vendors, which have thrived by focusing on deep, industry-specific functionality, flew under the radar while manufacturing software was a low priority. But they are now prime acquisition targets for the large automation and ERP vendors.

- ERP vendors—Infor, Oracle, QAD, and SAP are extending their products to provide deeper support for manufacturing operations, hoping to find more fertile ground and higher growth rates. While ERP has expanded well beyond core manufacturing resource planning (MRP II), financials, and logistics functionality into CRM, SCM, and PLM, the manufacturing shop floor is their least penetrated market.

Shifts in functionality

The globalization of manufacturing has highlighted major gaps in traditional manufacturing operations functionality, while also opening the door for a new breed of applications targeted beyond local site-based manufacturing operations and toward more far-reaching SNO. While traditional manufacturing operations is still required, and will likely be provided by the major automation vendors, SNO demands a new set of capabilities that may find a more appropriate home with the enterprise software hub of global manufacturers:

- EMI—Real-time performance management requires augmentation of business intelligence with EMI. In business terms, this is the contextualization of real-time manufacturing performance across distributed manufacturing sites.

- Supply sensing—Profitable demand-driven strategies require supply network modeling—that is, the supply sensing of the current inventory, work-in-process status, and capacity of raw materials, components, and product from suppliers and contract manufacturers.

- Global specification management—Customers expect consistent product quality, regardless of where products are designed and manufactured. Rising adoption of contract and offshore manufacturing requires global management of process and product and packaging specifications across both intra- and interorganizational boundaries. The need for master data management extends into manufacturing.

- Supply network genealogy—Beyond a common understanding of all design data associated with making products, global manufacturers have to track quality and as-built records for compliance reporting and enforcement across increasingly extended and dynamically reconfigurable supply networks.

- Operations process management (OPM)—The complementary, real-time equivalent of business process management, OPM starts with real-time event/services definition and monitoring, which requires complex aggregation and transformation of data from real-time shop-floor applications. It orchestrates many manufacturing workflows per second, using manufacturing service architectures (MSAs) exposed by the plethora of manufacturing software vendors. OPM and MSA allow abstraction and integration of manufacturing processes with BPM across application boundaries with the emerging enterprise services architectures of ERP.

Current and emerging business models

High systems and network availability, extremely high volumes of transactions, the need for predictable real-time performance, and considerable variability in manufacturing processes are some of the major barriers that face ERP vendors as they attempt to capture a share of the manufacturing operations application market. There has been no significant adoption of hosted manufacturing applications or SaaS. However, as global manufacturers attempt to capitalize on emerging manufacturing standards, such as ISA-95, and simplify their manufacturing application portfolios, companies are already moving toward enterprise-wide licensing of manufacturing software. This is a significant departure from the long, expensive pilots and site-by-site proofs and licensing that have hindered the survival and growth of small manufacturing software vendors.

Impact of new technology

BPM for building composite applications from enterprise systems has been a hot topic, but this emerging technology can't be used to orchestrate the manufacturing services that haven't been defined in highly standardized business applications. Manufacturing services need to be evaluated, triggered, and executed in real time. With no dominant manufacturing application software vendor in sight, most manufacturing processes will continue to be supported by composite applications that span a complex brew of best-of-breed point products. The emergence of OPM and MSAs will be vital to the sustained growth of the manufacturing software market.

Likely future

The market for manufacturing operations software is likely to grow over the next decade as North American manufacturers revitalize aging domestic facilities or shift investments to newer capacity being brought online in emerging industrial economies. Whether a handful of large software application providers can emerge to dominate this arena is today's multibillion-dollar question, as the split between traditional production operations and SNO creates potential opportunities for large automation and ERP providers alike.

Over the next three to five years, the boundaries between the local execution of manufacturing operations and the need to globally coordinate SNO will remain fluid, particularly as ERP vendors create service-based interfaces to external applications, and manufacturing operations vendors flesh out their own manufacturing service architectures. Many manufacturing software pure plays will be squeezed out by the massive software development and marketing budgets of ERP and large automation vendors.

In the near term, ERP vendors will attempt to capture strategic manufacturing segments by building out vertically integrated manufacturing functionality targeted at global coordination and local manufacturing execution, either through internal development efforts, partnerships, or acquisitions. Over the next three to five years, ERP vendors will have to support multiple manufacturing styles, add operational data stores, allow extensive customization of their user interfaces, and provide low-cost extensibility to retain the manufacturing foothold that they should capture in the next three years.

Retail Enterprise Applications

PART
ELEVEN

Anchored by core merchandise management, retail enterprise applications also include components that span corporate administration, advanced retail planning, store and cross-channel operations, and supply chain management. They are built on a modern technology infrastructure that manages master data, business intelligence, and internal and external integration. However, retailers are just starting to explore these retail ERP suites as foundational application platforms that support a wide range of business functions. Many still rely on independent infrastructures with scalable and open architectures to tie together their best-of-breed software portfolios. Whatever the approach, retailers are investing in packaged software that includes flexible data models to support a wide range of business functions throughout the retail enterprise.

Market size and growth rates

While companies in many other industries began investing in packaged software suites for their core business applications several years ago, most retailers have continued to rely on a jumble of legacy, custom, or best-of-breed applications to run their most critical operations. Many retail CIOs believed that it would be too difficult to rip out and replace their existing systems, and doubted any packaged retail applications were functionally rich enough to support their specific company needs. Research conducted by the National Retail Federation (NRF) and AMR Research found that just over half (52 percent) of the deployed enterprise retail applications among survey participants were built or maintained internally.

As such, retailer IT spending constituted 1.3 percent of revenue in 2005, with total IT budget increases of 7 percent projected for 2006. We reported in 2005 that the retail application market was expected to grow 10 percent from 2004 to $6.6 billion, with application license revenue accounting for nearly $2.2 billion. The retail application market is expected to grow incrementally by nearly $3.0 billion in the next four years to $9.3 billion in 2009.

Key players

Software companies and private equity firms are racing against Oracle and SAP to buy up hot retail software firms. With more than 30 deals totaling more than $4 billion in retail software company buyouts over the past few years, and with no signs of slowing, acquirers are jockeying to take advantage of the expected uptick in retailer spending as the retailers themselves benefit from the inflow of private equity capital. Top players are tackling the market from various directions.

Like SAP (purchasing Khimetrics and Triversity) and Oracle (purchasing Retek, ProfitLogic, 360Commerce, G-Log, and TempoSoft), other companies are growing through acquisitions, too. Most notably, Golden Gate Capital has compiled the likes of Ecometry, Blue Martini, ADS Retail, and GERS to form Escalate Retail. Manhattan Associates has moved beyond warehouse management with replenishment assets from Evant. Supply chain competitor RedPrairie has extended into the store with the purchase of BlueCube. And Sterling

Company Name	Revenue, 2004 ($M)	Revenue Forecast, 2005 ($M)	Revenue Share, 2004	Revenue Share Forecast, 2005	Growth Rate Forecast, 2004-2005
SAP	135	150	6%	7%	11%
SAS Institute	134	156	6%	7%	17%
Microsoft Business Solutions	125	144	6%	6%	15%
Oracle	119	202	6%	9%	70%
NCR/Teradata	105	113	5%	5%	8%
Retalix	85	130	4%	6%	53%
Retek	57	0	3%	0%	-100%
JDA Software	50	48	2%	2%	-4%
Kronos	42	46	2%	2%	10%
Sterling Commerce	39	46	2%	2%	18%
Subtotal	891	1036	42%	46%	16%
Total Retail Applications Market	2142	2242	100%	100%	5%

Retail applications vendors ranked by 2004 retail applications license and hosting revenue (incl. est. '05 growth)

221

Commerce acquired Yantra, expanding beyond infrastructure to provide applications that help retailers better manage order fulfillment and trading partner relationships.

Retail ERP players such as Aldata, JDA, Lawson, Oracle, Tomax, Retalix, and SAP are growing in popularity as retailers are seriously considering a move to integrated suites. Store operations technology is also in the spotlight. With a third of software application spending directed at point of sale (POS)-related software, vendors in this category, such as Datavantage, Epicor, Fujitsu, and NCR (including customer intelligence assets from Teradata), are growing in prominence. And workforce and task management vendors Kronos, Reflexis, StorePerform, and Workbrain are well positioned for increased store spending by retailers.

While Microsoft and IBM do not overtly sell software applications to Tier 1 retailers, they both play a major role in retail technology by providing broadly adopted infrastructure and integration technology.

Shifts in functionality

Global retailer dominance, blurred segments, channel obliteration, and consumer apathy continue to force retailers to rethink their business and IT strategies to avoid extinction. 2005 and 2006 retail IT spending insights show retailers are investing in technology that helps them better shape and fulfill consumer demand and deliver a superior shopping experience with flawless execution across all selling channels. In support of these initiatives, retailers will speed investment in commercially available software systems, which now provide powerful and flexible enough systems to replace home-built ones.

Applications focus on demand intelligence to better plan business from supplier to shelf. For the second straight year, retailers will spend on software that makes consumer demand insight and forecast analytics more prevalent and accessible throughout the organization. Insights generated from advanced planning systems will render antiquated reporting processes obsolete and allow for proactive, timely, and accurate decision-making. Demand-driven retailers will use software to help capture shopping insights from internal and external consumer behaviors and immediately respond with appropriate product assortments, optimal prices and promotions, and efficient store-centric stock levels.

An increasing number of software products has also been designed to help retailers create lifetime loyalty through better customer experiences. Software provides customer intelligence from cross-channel shopping interactions, gives access to product availability, ensures cost-effective order fulfillment, provides access to consistent product content, and aids the timely and relevant delivery of information to employees and customers.

Current and emerging business models

Most retail software vendors sell their own products through direct sales. Although resellers are not prominent, except for systems targeted at the small and midsize retailer, hardware vendors like Symbol, Intermec, Dell, and HP use value-added resellers. Customers purchase perpetual software licenses based primarily on the number of users and functional scope of the product.

Historically, retail service providers, including Accenture, BearingPoint, Capgemini, and Deloitte, would have significant influence on system selections, but there has been a shift in the past 18 months. Infrastructure vendors like Microsoft, IBM, and even SAP with NetWeaver are building a network of application partners that are certified on their platforms. With account control and strong relationships with retail executives, these technology providers have the ear of decision makers concerning technology investments.

Here are some of the other changes taking place in the market:

- Like other industries, software as a service will become a common purchasing option, and application hosting and managed services will become much more prevalent. SaaS today has low penetration in retail, but categories such as workforce and task management, e-commerce, and supply chain collaboration will likely be the first that retailers adopt.

- Service-oriented architectures have forced many retail ERP and best-of-breed vendors to sell applications and components based on industry standards. The ARTS data model, developed by the NRF, has helped give it momentum.

- The increase of web-based applications has replaced many legacy client/server deployments. In the retail environment, with many dispersed selling locations, this has allowed retailers to manage data and software centrally and access it through a browser. Growing investments in more robust broadband connectivity ensure speed and reliability in the network. It is important to note that home office/headquarter applications for retail planning, finance, and marketing have remained in the traditional architecture.

Impact of new technology

New technology is allowing retailers to accomplish the following:

- Business flexibility—Enterprise systems let retailers quickly respond to changing market conditions, support new organizational initiatives, gain the visibility and reporting control required to comply with regulations, and begin to move retailers away from expensive and risky legacy infrastructures that limit category and geographic expansion.

- Central management of information—By the end of 2007, retailers anticipate that 76 percent of store software applications will be physically hosted and managed centrally at a company-owned or third-party data center. While retailers are still reluctant to move core POS software off store servers, newer versions of software applications, such as workforce and task management, customer loyalty, inventory, and order management, are conducive to central management. When data and processes are managed centrally and accessed through thin-client technology, it usually reduces software maintenance costs, overall capital investment, and technical integration costs. The strategy also allows retailers to manage their businesses more holistically and allow for a more unified relationship with customers across various channels.

- Cross-channel maturity—Limitations of first-generation e-commerce systems are forcing retailers to invest in next-generation systems to create consistent, cross-channel processes and abilities. To do this, retailers are replacing existing e-commerce software with new e-commerce business-to-consumer (B2C) platforms that integrate seamlessly with the rest of the company's operations. These platforms bridge customer interactions among every touchpoint by embedding cross-channel abilities into merchandising, supply chain, and store processes.

- Increased usability—To ensure adoption and maximum value of any application, whether in the supply chain, merchandise planning, or store operations, usability and ease of implementation has become a guiding principle for every selection.

Likely future

The more than 30 deals totaling more than $4 billion in retail software company buyouts over the past two years demonstrate that companies are fighting for this significant market opportunity. Consolidation is far from over.

In all of the retail software consolidation frenzy, retailers themselves can't be forgotten. Firms must deliver value versus making investment bankers and software vendors wealthier. Retailers are getting tired of all the acquisitions and want to start hearing how it benefits them and the consumer. To ensure this will happen, expect software vendor investments to increase usability, embed analytics, become more flexible and configurable, become better integrated among acquired or built functionality, and provide a complete view of customer and product information.

Acronyms and Initialisms

3PL	Third-party logistics	EAI	Enterprise application integration
A&D	Aerospace and defense		
APC	Advanced process control	EAM	Enterprise asset management
APO	Advanced planning and optimization	EDA	Electronic design automation
APS	Advanced planning and scheduling or advanced process simulation	EDI	Electronic data interchange
ARB	Architecture review board	EDW	Electronic data warehouse
ASN	Advanced shipping notice	EMI	Enterprise manufacturing intelligence
ASP	Application service provider	ERP	Enterprise resource planning
B2B	Business to business	ESB	Enterprise service bus
B2C	Business to consumer	GSM	Global specifications management
BAM	Business activity monitoring	HCM	Human capital management
BI	Business intelligence	HMI	Human-machine interface
BPEL	Business process execution language	HR	Human resources
BPM	Business process management	IM	Instant messaging
BPO	Business process outsourcing	IPO	Initial public offering
CAD	Computer-aided design	IT	Information technology
CAGR	Compound annual growth rate	ITIL	IT infrastructure library
CDI	Customer data integration	KPI	Key performance indicator
CNM	Customer needs management	LIMS	Laboratory information management system
CPD	Collaborative product-process design	M&A	Merger and acquisition
CRM	Customer relationship management	MDM	Master data management
		MES	Manufacturing execution system
DDSN	Demand-driven supply network	MESA	Multi-enterprise services architecture
DMS	Direct material sourcing	MRO	Maintenance, repair, and overhaul

MRP	Materials requirements planning	S&OP	Sales and operations planning
MRP II	Manufacturing resource planning	SaaS	Software as a service
MSA	Manufacturing service architecture	SCADA	Supervisory control and data acquisition
MTOM	Message Transmission Optimization Mechanism	SCM	Supply chain management
		SCP	Supply chain planning
NPDI	New product development and introduction	SFA	Sales force automation
		SI	System integrator
		SLA	Service-level agreement
NRF	National Retail Federation	SLM	Service lifecycle management
NSR	Navigation, search, and retrieval	SMB	Small and midsize business
OEM	Original equipment manufacturer	SMI	Supplier-managed inventory
		SNO	Supply network operations
OPM	Operations process management	SOA	Service-oriented architecture
PBF	Planning, budgeting, and forecasting	SOAP	Simple object access protocol
PDM	Product data management	SOX	Sarbanes-Oxley Act
PLM	Product lifecycle management	SPC	Statistical process control
		SPL	Service parts logistics
PM	Performance management	SPM	Supplier performance management
POS	Point of sale		
PPM	Product portfolio management	SRM	Supplier relationship management
QMS	Quality management system	TCO	Total cost of ownership
		VAN	Value-added network
R&D	Research and development	VC	Venture capital
RDF	Resource description framework	VMI	Vendor-managed inventory
RDL	Resource description language	VoIP	Voice over Internet protocol
RFID	Radio frequency identification	WMS	Warehouse management system
RFP	Request for proposal	WSDL	Web services description language
RFQ	Request for quotation	XML	Extensible markup language

Index

A

ABB, 214
Accenture, 22, 125, 223
  global delivery models, 129
Acquisitions
  Consolidation customer
    base and, 23–24
Activant, 173
Actuate, 164
Adage, 17
ADS Retail, 220
Agile Software, 206
Aldata, 222
Amazon.com, 52
amdocs, 187
Architecture hybrid-tenancy
  model, 112–113
    multitenancy model,
      111–112
Architecture review board
  SOA and, 76
Ariba, 203
  supply management segment,
    180, 181
Astea, 193, 194
AT Kearney, 180, 181
Authoria, 158
Autodesk, 207
Axway, 200, 201

B

Baan, 206
Battery Ventures VI, 18
BearingPoint, 129, 223
Best-of-breed segment
  Internet bubble and, 8
  what happened to, 7–8
Big Four
  stability of, for customers,
    26–27

Blogs
  customer service and
    self-service, 52
  definition and characteristics
    of, 48
  employee learning and human
    capital management, 53
  executive alignment and
    corporate communication,
    51
  IT change management,
    project tracking and
    documentation, 51
  in knowledge management
    paradox, 49–50
  supplier and partner
    collaboration, 53
  using in enterprise, 50–53
Blue Martini, 220
BlueCube, 158, 222
BRAIN, 17
Business intelligence (BI) and
  performance management
    (PM), 163–169
  current and emerging
    business models, 167–168
  future of, 169
  impact of new technology,
    168–169
  key players, 164–166
  market size and growth
    rates, 164
  overview of, 163–164
  revenue, 165
  shifts in functionality,
    166–167
Business management
  in SLM, 192
Business Objects, 164

Business process consulting
  maturity model, 125–126
Business process management
  Owens & Minor example, 43
  Sarbanes-Oxley Act, 41–42
  service-oriented architecture
    and, 40–42
Business process outsourcing
  private equity firms
    acquisitions, 22
Business service management
  SOA transition and, 79
Business-to-business (B2B)
  e-business, 199–204
    current and emerging
      business models,
      201–203
    future, 204
    impact of new technology,
      203
    key players, 200
    market size and growth
      rates, 200
    overview of, 199
    shifts in functionality, 201

C
Cadence, 207
Capgemini, 129, 223
Centra, 158
Cerberus, 23
Change management
  SOA and, 78
Click Commerce, 193, 194
Click2Learn, 158
ClickSoftware, 193, 194
Cognizant, 128
Cognos, 164
Commerce One, 8
Communications convergence
  Web 2.0, 57

Compliance
  Sarbanes-Oxley Act, 41–42
Composite application
  snap-on approach of
    small vendors, 29
Consolidation
  ERP vendors and, 9
  new business strategies
    and, 19–22
  private equity firms and, 15–24
Content management software
  VC and private equity
    investment in, 20–21
Convergence
  unbound portal, 66
Corporate communication
  using blogs and wikis, 51
CSC, 129
Customer relationship
  management (CRM), 185–190
    current and emerging
      business models, 188–189
    future, 190
    impact of new technology,
      189
    key players, 186–187
    market size and
      growth rates, 186
    overview of, 185
    SaaS and, 108
    shifts in functionality,
      186, 188
    VC and private equity
      investment in, 20–21
Customer service
  using blogs and wikis, 52
Customers
  acquisitions and customer base,
    23–24
  customer-oriented SOA
    deployment, 83–84

multitenancy vs. hybrid-
 tenancy model, 111–113
 stability of Big Four, 26–27
Customization
 buyer decisions on, 114
 SOA and, 85–86
CVS, 22
Cyclone Commerce, 201

D

Dassault Systemes, 206
Data transformation
 SOA and, 73
Datavantage, 222
Dell, 223
Deloitte, 22, 223
 global delivery models, 129
Demand-driven supply networks
 web services impact on, 58
Demand management
 SOA and, 78
Demantra, 172
Dendrite, 187
Descartes, 201
Design for service, 197
DHL
 integration complexity and
  business agility, 37–38
 using SOA, 37–38
Docent, 158
Duffield, Dave, 141

E

E2open, 200, 201, 202
EAI, 202
EasyLink Services, 200
Ecometry, 220
ecVision, 180
EDS, 129
Emerson, 214
Employee learning
 using blogs and wikis, 53

Emptoris, 180
Enrich
 in service enablement layer, 90
Enterprise applications
 destroying its fragile
  ecosystem, 7–13
 historical perspective, VII–VIII
 predictions of future of,
  135–143
Enterprise architecture
 clearly define for SOA
  transition, 78
Enterprise manufacturing
 intelligence (EMI), 215
Enterprise resource planning.
 See also ERP
Entrepreneurs
 commercializing innovation,
  25–26
 getting started, 11–12
 view of venture capital, 12
Epicor, 9, 151, 222
ePlus, 180
Eqos, 180
ERP
 model-based applications
  based on SOA, 141–142
 next-generation infrastructure
  and, 140–141
 recycle over buying new, 142
 total cost of ownership, 140
ERP vendors, 149–153
 building ecosystem of
  independent software
  companies, 10–13
 caution for multiple service
  provider strategy, 123
 concentration of revenue and
  lack of innovation, 10–13
 consolidation and, 9
 current and emerging business
  models, 152–153

dynamics that influence
number of service providers,
122
future of, 153
impact of new technology, 153
Indian firms as, 125–130
Internet bubble and, 8
key players, 150–151
market size and growth rates,
150
multiple-source service provider
strategy, 122–123
overview of, 149
revenue of, 151
SaaS and, 109
shifts in functionality, 150, 152
single-source service provider
strategy, 122
spending on, 121
Escalate Retail, 220
Executives
using blogs and wikis, 51

F

Francisco Partners, 17, 18
Freeborders, 180
Fujitsu, 222

G

G-Log, 172, 220
GE Fanuc, 214
Geac, 25, 151
General Atlantic Partners, 23
Gerber Technology, 207
GERS, 220
Gerstner, Lou, XII
GetSilicon, 201
Global delivery models, 129
Global specification management,
215
Golden Gate Capital, 17, 18, 23,
24, 220

Google, 57
Governance hurdle for SOA, 72,
75–79, 87–91
Great Plains, 24
Greenough, Mike, 24
GXS, 200

H

HCL Technologies, 129
Healthcare software
VC and private equity
investment in, 20–21
Hire.com, 158
Honeywell, 214
Horn, Paul, 140–141
HP, 223
global delivery models, 129
Hubspan, 202
Human capital management
(HCM), 155–161
current and emerging
business models, 159–160
impact of new technology,
160
key players in, 156–158
market size and growth
rates, 156
overview of, 155–156
revenue, 157
shifts in functionality,
158–159
using blogs and wikis, 53
VC and private equity
investment in, 20–21
Hybrid-tenancy model, 112–113
Hyperion Solutions, 164

I

i2, 8, 181, 202
SCM segment, 173–174
IBM, XI, 11, 22, 125, 222, 223

BI/PM segment, 166
global delivery models, 129
as part of Big Four and
customer preference of,
26–27
IBS
SCM segment, 172, 173
supply management segment,
180, 181
ICG Commerce, 180
Identity
unbound portal, 65
IEX, 159
IFS, 193, 194
Independent software companies
ERP vendors building
partnerships with, 10–13
innovation and, 11–13
Indian firms
in business process consulting
maturity model, 125–126
future labor supply, 130
global delivery models, 129
infrastructure problems, 130
services provided by, 127–128
strategic enterprise application
services by, 128
Indus, 193, 194
Infor, 9, 24, 173, 214
in ERP segment, 150, 151
private equity firm
consolidation, 17
Information Builders, 164
Information in context, 166
Information technology
outsourcing
private equity firm
acquisitions, 22
Information to the masses, 166
Infosys, 127
Infrastructure standards
innovation and, 11

Innovation
commercializing, 25–26
future of, XI–XIII
infrastructure standards, 11
loss of, and independent
software companies, 11–13
sources of, 11
startups and, 11–12
Inovis, 200
Intentia, 151
Intermec, 223
Internet bubble
specialty vendors and, 8
Invensys, 214
Investment planning
SOA and, 77
IPO
small vendors and, 27
software companies and, 23
IT
impact of SOA on, 77–78
spending on, 26–27
using blogs and wikis, 51
Iterative development
SOA and, 76

J
JD Edwards, 8, 9, 156, 172
JDA, 221, 222
Jesta, 180

K
Kaba Benzing, 157
Kenexa, 158
Khimetrics, 220
Knowledge management paradox
blogs and wikis in, 49–50
Kronos, 158, 221, 222
in HCM segment, 157–158

L

Lane, Ray, 9
Lawson, 9, 222
  in ERP segment, 150, 151
  in HCM segment, 157
  in SLM segment, 193, 194
Lectra Systems, 207
Licensing and maintenance
  policies. *See also* Software as a
  service (SaaS)
    buyers' differing preferences
      for fee structure, 99–100
    executives' attitude toward,
      97–99
    future changes in, 103
    on-demand approach,
      99–100, 103, 106–107
    rising rates for maintenance,
      102–103
    site licensing, 99–100
    third-party support growth,
      100–101

M

Maintenance and operations
  SOA and, 78
Manhattan Associates, 172, 173,
  174, 220
Mann, Darlene, 11–12
Manufacturing operations
  segment, 211–218
    current and emerging
      business models, 216
    future, 217–218
    impact of new technology,
      217
    key players, 214
    market size and growth
      rates, 212–213
    overview of, 211–212
    shifts in functionality,
      215–216

Manugistics, 25, 173
Master data management (MDM),
  91
MatrixOne, 206
MCA Solutions, 193
Mentor Graphics, 207
Message Transmission
  Optimization Mechanism
  (MTOM), 74
Metrix, 193, 194
Microsoft, 11, 24, 222, 223
  in BI/PM segment, 166
  in CRM segment, 186, 187
  in ERP segment, XI, 150, 151
  in HCM segment, 157
  as part of Big Four and
    customer preference of,
    26–27
  percent of industry profit, 9
MicroStrategy, 164
Midmarket
  SOA benefits for, 45–46
Model-based applications based on
  SOA, 141–142
MSC Software, 207
Multitenancy model, 111–112

N

Navigation, search, and retrieval,
  57
Navision, 24
NCR, 221, 222
NetWeaver, 223
NGC, 180
NICE Systems, 159
Nistevo, 201

O

Offshore
  meaninglessness of, 129–130
Operations process management
  216

Optimization projects
  by Indian firms, 128
Oracle, XI, 10, 24, 42, 141
  in BI/PM segment, 164, 166
  in CRM segment, 186, 187
  in ERP segment, 150–151
  in HCM segment, 156–157
  in manufacturing operations,
    214
  market share, 9
  as part of Big Four and
    customer preference of,
    26–27
  in PLM segment, 206
  in retail enterprise applications,
    220, 221
  in SCM segment, 172–173
  in SLM segment, 193, 194
  supply management segment,
    180, 181
  using SOA, 39–40
Outsourcing
  acquisitions and private
    equity firms, 22
Owens & Minor
  SOA and BPM, 43

P
Partnerships
  using blogs and wikis, 53
Pathlore, 158
Patni, 127
PeopleSoft, 8, 9, 24, 25, 141, 156,
    164, 172
Perfect Commerce, 180, 203
Performance indicator monitoring,
    89
Performix, 159
Plumtree, 62
Portals
  as competitive battlefront,
    62–63

service-oriented architecture
    and, 61
  unbound, 63–66
Portfolio management
  SOA and, 76, 78
Presence, unbound portal, 66
Private equity firms
  advantages/disadvantages of, 16
  customer bases and
    acquisitions, 23–24
  exit strategy and, 23–24
  helping reform software
    market, 24
  major players, 17–18
  new business strategies and,
    19–22
  outsourcing and, 22
  segment investments, 20–21
  trend toward consolidation
    and, 15–17
Process hurdle of SOA, 81–86 .
Process improvement
  Sarbanes-Oxley Act, 41–42
Process modeling, 89
Procurement. *See* Supply
    management
Procuri, 180
Product lifecycle management
    (PLM), 205–209
  current and emerging
    business models,
    208–209
  future, 209
  impact of new technology,
    209
  key players, 206–207
  market size and growth
    rates, 206
  overview of, 205
  revenue, 207
  shifts in functionality, 206,
    208

VC and private equity
investment in, 20–21
ProfitLogic, 220
Project tracking
using blogs and wikis, 51
PTC, 206, 207

Q

QAD, 214

R

RedPrairie, 158, 173, 222
Reflexis, 222
Resource description language, 74
Retail enterprise applications,
219–225
current and emerging
business models,
223–224
future, 225
impact of new technology,
224–225
key players, 220–222
market size and growth
rates, 220
overview of, 219
revenue, 221
shifts in functionality,
222–223
Retalix, 221, 222
Retek, 172, 220, 221
Rich client support, 57
Richardson, Bruce, IX, 133,
139–143
RightNow
CRM segment, 186, 187
Rockwell, 214

S

Saba, 158
Sage Group

in ERP segment, 150, 151
in HCM segment, 157
salesforce.com, 107, 108, 188
in CRM segment, 186, 187
SAP, XI, 10, 141
in BI/PM segment, 164
in CRM segment, 186, 187
in ERP segment, 150–151
in HCM segment, 156–157
in manufacturing operations,
214
market share, 9
as part of Big Four and
customer preference of,
26–27
in PLM segment, 206, 207
in retail enterprise applications,
220, 221
in SCM segment, 172–173
in SLM segment, 193, 194
in supply management segment,
180, 181
using SOA, 39–40
Sarbanes-Oxley Act, 41–42
SAS Institute, 164
Satyam, 128
Search engines
Web 2.0, 57
Search for right information,
167
Security
SOA and, 73, 78
Security software
VC and private equity
investment in, 20–21
SEEBURGER, 200, 202
Self-service
using blogs and wikis, 52
Semantic web, 57
Service discovery, 191–192
Service enablement layer, 90–91
Service fulfillment, 192

Service knowledge, 192
Service lifecycle management
(SLM), 191–198
    categories of, 191–192
    current and emerging
        business models, 196
    future, 197–198
    impact of new technology,
        197
    key players, 193–194
    market size and growth rate,
        193
    overview of, 191–192
    shifts in functionality,
        195–196
Service-oriented architecture
(SOA)
    aligned incentives, 76, 79
    architecture review board, 76
    benefits for midmarket,
        45–46
    business process
        management and, 40–42
    change management, 78
    characteristics of, 35–36
    choices for companies,
        44–45
    customer oriented, 83–84
    customizations and, 85–86
    data transformation, 73
    defined, 35–36
    DHL example, 37–38
    effect on application market,
        39–40
    governance hurdle, 72,
        75–79, 87–91
    Indian firms role in,
        125–130
    investment planning, 77
    iterative development, 76
    maintenance and operations,
        78

new software development
    model, 72
new testing requirements,
    76, 79
Oracle and SAP using,
    39–40
overview of hurdles for,
    71–74
Owens & Minor example,
    43
portals and, 61
portfolio management, 76
preparing for transition to,
    78–79
process hurdle, 81–86
recommendations for, 45
Sarbanes-Oxley Act and,
    41–42
security, 73, 78
service enablement layer,
    90–91
service policy management,
    72
service repositories, 73
software development, 77
technology and governance
    hurdle, 87–91
technology-governance
    framework, 87–89
in warehouse management
    systems, 85–86
web services impact on, 58
Service-oriented technique, 83
Service parts management, 197
Service policy management
    SOA and, 72
Service providers
    dynamics that influence
        numbers of, 122
    single vs. multiple-source
        strategy, 122–123

Service repositories
  SOA and, 73
ServiceBench, 193, 194
Servigistics, 159, 193, 194
Shepherd, Jim, 133, 135–138
Siebel, 9, 156, 164
  CRM segment, 186, 187
Siemens, 214
Silver Oak Solutions, 180
Simple object access protocol
  (SOAP), 74
Single-source service provider
  strategy, 122–123
Siperian, 11
Small vendors
  characteristics of successful,
    28–29
  customer preference for Big
    Four, 26–27
  IPO or acquisition exit options
    for, 27–28
  as service driven, 28
  snap-on approach, 29
  sustainability of, 28
SmartTime, 158
Snap-on approach
  of small vendors, 29
Social networking
  Web 2.0, 58
Software
  model-based applications based
    on SOA, 141–142
Software as a service (SaaS)
  actual use of, 106–107
  cost elements of, 115
  customization decisions for
    buyer, 114
  effects on software industry
    landscape, 108–109
  future of, 116
  historical perspective on, 105
  hybrid-tenancy model, 112–113

multitenancy model, 111–112
users interest in, 106–107
vendors difficulties with,
  107–108
web services impact on, 58
Software development
  SOA and new model for, 72,
    75–77
  upgrades and SaaS, 109
Sourcing. *See* Supply management
Specialty vendors
  effect of consolidation, 9
  Internet bubble and, 8
  what happened to, 7–8
SSA Global, 23, 151
Startups
  characteristics for successful,
    28–29
  SaaS and, 108
Sterling Commerce, 200, 201,
  220, 222
StorePerform, 222
SuccessFactors, 158
SumTotal, 158
Supplier performance portals, 83,
  84
Suppliers
  SOA deployment for better
    collaboration, 83–84
  using blogs and wikis, 53
Supply chain management (SCM),
  171–177
  current and emerging
    business models, 175–176
  future of, 177
  impact of new technology,
    176–177
  key players, 172–174
  market size and growth
    rates, 172
  overview of, 171–172
  revenue, 173

shifts in functionality,
174–175
Supply chain market
SaaS and, 109
Supply management, 179–184
current and emerging business
models, 182–183
future, 184
impact of new technology, 183
key players, 180, 181
market size and growth rates,
180
overview of, 179
shifts in functionality, 180, 182
Supply network genealogy, 215
Supply sensing, 215
Sustainability
of small vendors, 28
Swisslog, 173
Symbol, 223
Systems management software
VC and private equity
investment in, 20–21

T

Taleo, 157
Tata Consultancy Services (TCS),
128
TempoSoft, 220
Teradata, 221
Testing
new testing requirement and
SOA transition, 76, 79
Third-party support, 100–101
Thoma Cressey Equity Partners,
17, 18
360Commerce, 220
Tomax, 222
TomorrowNow, 100
Tourtellotte Solutions, 180

TR2, 201
Tradestone, 180
Transact
in service enablement layer, 90
TransDecisions, 159
Triversity, 220

U

UGS, 206, 207
Ultimate Software, 157
Unbound portal, 63–66
convergence, 66
identity, 65
presence, 66
Unicru, 158
Upgrades
SaaS and, 109
Usage-based pricing. *See* Software
as a service (SaaS)

V

Vendor-managed inventory (VMI)
systems, 83, 84
Vendors
difficulties with SaaS, 107–108
ownership of and private equity
firms, 15–24
portal as competitive
battlefront, 62–63
Venture capital
entrepreneurs' anti-VC attitude,
12
Internet bubble and specialty
vendors, 8
loss of interest in enterprise
application, 10–11, 12
segment investments, 20–21
statistics on investments of, 19
Web 2.0, 12
Vertical Solutions, 193, 194

W

W3C, 74
Warehouse management systems
  SOA in, 85–86
Web 2.0, 55–59, 140–141
  characteristics of, 55–56
  evolving aspects of, 56–58
  impact of web on business
    initiatives, 58
  media and communications
    convergence, 57
  navigation, search and retrieval,
    57
  rich client support, 57
  semantic web, 57
  social networking techniques,
    58
  venture capital, 12
  web data mining and
    analytics, 58
Web 3.0, 59
Web data mining and analytics
  Web 2.0, 58
Web service standards, 74
Web services description language
  (WSDL), 74
Webhire, 158
webMethods, 200
Wikis
  customer service and
    self-service, 52
  definition and characteristics
    of, 48
  employee learning and human
    capital management, 53
  executive alignment and
    corporate communication,
    51
  IT change management, project
    tracking and
    documentation, 51
  in knowledge management
    paradox, 49–50
  supplier and partner
    collaboration, 53
  using in enterprise, 50–53
Wipro, 127
Wireless software
  VC and private equity
    investment in, 20–21
Wookey, John, 141
Workbrain, 157, 222
Workday, 141
WS, 74

Y

Yahoo!, 57
Yantra, 201, 222

Z

Zencke, Peter, 141
Zymmetry, 180

Contributors

The following people contributed to the content of this book:
Greg Aimi, Rob Bois, Mike Burkett, Marianne D'Aquila, Christa Degnan Manning, Ian Finley, Jeff Freyermuth, Rob Garf, Dennis Gaughan, John Hagerty, Mark Hillman, Steve Hochman, Simon Jacobson, Eric Karofsky, Colin Masson, Laura McCaughey, Jim Murphy, Mickey North Rizza, Derek Prior, Fenella Sirkisoon, Alison Smith, Dana Stiffler, and Bill Swanton.

About AMR Research

Research and Advice That Matter

AMR Research is the No. 1 advisory firm focused on the intersection of business process with supply chain and ERP. Founded in 1986, we provide subscription advisory services and peer networking opportunities to operations and IT executives in the consumer products, life sciences, manufacturing, and retail sectors.

Since 1995, we have published over 14,000 pieces of research. Our analysts focus on delivering independent, leading-edge research on both established and emerging technologies. This analysis is supported by daily interaction with the most extensive network of market contacts and the best quantitative data in the industry.

125 Summer Street
Fourth Floor
Boston, MA 02110
Tel: +1-617-542-6600
Fax: +1-617-542-5670

555 Montgomery Street
Suite 650
San Francisco, CA 94111
Tel: +1-415-217-3737

Parkshot House
5 Kew Road
Richmond, Surrey
TW9 2PR
United Kingdom
Tel: +44 (0) 20 8334 8090
Fax: +44 (0) 20 8334 8190

Colophon

The interior pages of *The Future of Enterprise Applications* were printed on Mohawk Options 100% PC Cream White and the cover on Mohawk Options 100% PC Cool White Smooth. Both are made with 100% post-consumer waste fiber and manufactured with renewable, non-polluting, wind-generated electricity.

The body text typeface is Adobe Garamond Pro, designed by Robert Slimbach. The headings, chapter titles, figures, and tables use the typeface Duty, designed by Lee Fasciani.

The original design of this book was done by Jason Warriner (www.jaywar.com).

Angela Tavares, Joseph Neylon, Jason Leary, and Mike Brown did the proofreading, layout, and production work.

Supply Chain Saves the World
An AMR Research Publication

Making money and saving the world at the same time is the next frontier. The supply chain revolution is making all of this possible—and profitable. Drawing on two decades of analysis, AMR Research shares this opportunity for supply chain and technology professionals to make a difference for their companies and for the world.

"AMR Research's work on the global supply chain is driving change in business and is something from which leading companies can certainly benefit. Equally interesting is how the book demonstrates the way this relatively new discipline is being used to solve world problems."
—**Stu Reed, Executive Vice President, Integrated Supply Chain, Motorola, Inc.**

"AMR Research describes a new way of doing business, a new model that IBM calls the globally integrated enterprise. And fundamentally, it all starts with the supply chain, which can be the catalyst to integrate operations and production to deliver value to clients worldwide."
—**Bob Moffat, Senior Vice President, Integrated Operations, IBM Corporation**

"An innovative book showing how supply chain concepts can help both companies and society grapple with the challenges of globalization, environmental sustainability, and world health. Supply chain management has come a long way!"
—**Warren H. Hausman, Department of Management Science and Engineering, Stanford University**